Choose Your Own Minecraft Story

The Zombie Adventure 2:

Journey to the Ender

John Diary

For all the incredible readers. I do it for you.

And, of course, for Sarah.

Hey!

It's me, John Diary, the author. Before you get started, I wanted to tell you something very important.

This book is no normal book! In this book, you, not the author, get to decide what happens next. Start reading it like normal but at the end of each section you will get two or more choices of what you can do next. Choose what you want to do next and then turn to the appropriate page to keep reading.

DON'T just flip through the pages of the book, because that will ruin the surprise! And also it won't make any sense!

There are thirty different endings in this book and three "happy" endings that will lead you to the next book. Once you get to one ending, go back and start reading again. There are so many stories in this one book!

ALSO, this is a sequel to Choose Your Own Minecraft Story: The Zombie Adventure. Three endings in that book lead to the beginning of this one. If you haven't found those endings yet, go back and find them! But if you haven't read the book, that's okay too. Start here! You'll figure it out.

Happy reading,

John

Chosen One?

The words bounce around the inside of your head. What does he mean? You stare up at the Elder Golem whose stone face doesn't make his words any less mysterious.

Chosen One?

It had been a pretty confusing day. Probably the most confusing day in your whole life. You'd woken up as a zombie. And not just any zombie. A zombie in a game… A zombie in *Minecraft*. You'd been hurried out the door by a bossy skeleton who apparently could talk?! That was confusing enough. And you'd met creepers who apparently didn't want to blow up players but just got so excited about being around them that they literally blew up. *Very* confusing. And then you'd been told some confusing story about someone who'd gotten stuck in the game before and been confusingly brought to this place, with this monstrous golem who was supposed to help you get home.

And somehow, him saying *'Chosen One'* was still the most confusing thing that had happened all day.

Well if not the *most* confusing. At least a very close second.

Maybe he'd made a mistake. Maybe you'd misheard him. Maybe he'd said *'frozen bun'* or *'Cho and Juan'* or *'crows in nun'*. Actually… now that you think about it, that might be *more* confusing.

"Excuse me, Mister Golem," you say, "did you just say *Chosen One?*"

The golem raises one massive, stony eyebrow and frowns. It makes the sound of a small earthquake.

"Oh no," you panic, "was it 'frozen bun'?"

He doesn't look very impressed.

"Ha, ha," you say nervously. "No, of course it was 'Cho and Juan'. Duh."

Both his mossy eyebrows narrow to a point in the middle of his forehead. It makes the noise of a slightly bigger earthquake.

What was he thinking?, you ask yourself silently. It is impossible to read that big, stony face.

Slowly the golem opens his big mouth to speak. "Who's Juan?" he says with a voice of pouring gravel.

You squint at him, not knowing what to say.

After a second, he gets over it. With an ear-splitting grinding noise, the elder golem turns on his heel. "Come Chosen One, there's no time to waste. We have to send you home," he says and begins to walk off. Each step vibrates the ground beneath your feet.

If you tell the golem you're not the 'Chosen One', *turn to page 6.*

If you follow him, *turn to page 9.*

Don't panic, you think to yourself. *You're not a player, remember? To them you're just another zombie. Stay cool and think… zombie-ish thoughts.*

You try thinking about rotting flesh and brains. You think about making really freaky sounds to terrify players while they're trying to mine. Just classic zombie stuff.

The zombies lumber towards you.

"Hey, hey guys," you say, trying not to sound as nervous as you are. "How're you guys doing?"

"*GRauuuUUUUUURGH!*" one zombie says while lurching right at you. And while you *hear* '*GRauuuUUUUUURGH*' you understand something totally different: "Hey buddy! How's it going! You almost missed the meeting!"

You blink a couple times. *A meeting? Buddy?*

"Uh, hey," you say, once you get it together. "Good, I'm good… buddy."

"*GRAAAAAuuuungggggg!*" another zombie says. He's right on top of you and he has his arms out like he's about to attack! But before you can run you realize he's just saying "Come in for a hug!"

He comes at you with his arms outstretched and wraps them right around you.

"Friend!" he says in zombie groans.

"Oh hey," you say, completely surprised.

The zombie stops hugging you and takes a step back, staring at you. He looks stern… Have you done something wrong?

"Why don't you hug me back?" the zombie asked.

"Oh, uh, sorry. I'm just…" You try to think of an excuse. "Having a bad day," you say.

"All the more reason for hugs!" The zombie leans in again and wraps his big arms around you, squeezing tight. You hug back, just trying to avoid trouble. He smells a bit bad. You don't complain though. You probably don't smell great yourself.

The zombie backs away and you're a little relieved that the hugging is done. And then the first zombie that spoke lurches towards you and wraps his arms around you too.

"Oh, uh, okay," you say. "Another hug? Very generous."

After a long couple seconds, he backs off and you open your mouth. "Hey guys, I was wondering if—"

But you're immediately smothered by yet *another* zombie hugging you tight.

After five more hugs, they've all gotten a chance, and they seem to be happy. Finally, you can speak.

"Hey guys, I was wondering if you could help me," you say.

They nod their heads slowly, but excitedly. "Anything for our brother!"

You smile nervously. "Okay, great. I'm looking for a… room with lava. Have you seen a room like that?"

"With lava?" one zombie asks.

"In here?" another asks.

"Of course!" a third zombie exclaims.

"Come, come, we'll show you." And just like that, you are herded off by eight zombies through the maze of rooms that make up the stronghold. As you waddle together, the zombies talk excitedly. They ask you where you're from and how many people you've eaten and who tasted the best. You try your best to make up some convincing answers.

You say that you once had a really delicious player dressed in diamond armour and they all look at you a bit weird.

"Huh," one says. "But everyone knows noobs taste the best. That's weird…"

They slow down and stop to look at you.

"Oh! Yeah! Of course!" you say. "Everyone knows that… He *was* a noob. He just found some armour somewhere. In a chest. Got lucky."

The zombies all relaxed and kept walking. "Oh, of course, of course."

That was a close one!

Soon they stop in front of a door.

"Right through there, buddy!" one says. "Have a great time!"

You thank them and promise that you will. You push through the door and close it carefully behind you.

There it is. There's a staircase leading up and over a pool of lava that dominates half the room. It's *hot* in here. Something strange is floating above the pool… it's a circle of stones with open holes in them.

Strange.

The golem said to call for him when you found it, but maybe it wouldn't hurt just to examine the strange circle first…

If you call for the golem, *turn to page 15.*

If you examine the stone circle, *turn to page 31.*

"Hey!" you say, shouting to be heard over the golem's thundering footsteps. "I think you're confused. I'm not who you think I am!"

The golem stops walking, causing another shockwave that almost knocks you off your feet. He turns his head to you, but when you think the head will stop turning, it doesn't, it just keeps going. It pivots its head all the way around so that it's totally backwards on its body.

You scrunch up your little green nose. *Gross.*

"What?" the golem booms.

"I, uh, I'm not who you think I am…" This time you don't say it with quite the same confidence.

"What?" the golem repeats.

You thought that this golem was supposed to be very wise. You thought that it was supposed to have been around forever. It doesn't seem that bright…

"Okay, well you said— you called me the Chosen One, and that's just not true. I don't know who you think I am or what you think I'm doing here. But I have bad news…" You take a deep breath. "I'm just a kid who was playing Minecraft for too long and fell asleep on my keyboard and when I woke up in the morning, well I woke up like *this.*" You point up and down your weird, green, zombie body. "I'm not some sort of hero or something…"

"Hmm, I see," said the golem. "So you don't think that you're the Chosen One?"

"No, definitely not," you say shortly.

"Have you heard the prophecy?" the golem asked, but before you could answer, he asked you another question. "Have you lived on this server for years and years? Do you know the secrets of the portals? Do you know how this world began? Have you stood on this place since the beginning of time and watched this world morph and move around you?"

Woah.

"Uh, no," you say. "No."

"Well," the golem said in the same monotone voice. "I have. So which of us do you think is more likely to know if you're the Chosen One or not?"

Well, maybe he has a point… Your brain is spinning.

Without saying another word, the golem turned his head back around and started walking again. "Quickly, small green one," he said. "Come if you're the Chosen One. And if you're not, I can't help you. You might as well stay here."

If you go with the golem, *turn to page 12.*

If you stay put, *turn to page 10.*

Right.

Right feels… well, right. You turn the handle of the door awkwardly with your decaying zombie hands and stumble forward into the dark. Your zombie eyes peer through the darkness at a gloomy room in front of you.

There's not much in it. Just some cobwebs and a chest in the corner. Normally a chest would fill you with excitement, but what does a zombie want with a chest? There are two doors in this room also.

The sound of zombie moans can be heard coming distantly through the door on your right. Everything seems quiet on the left.

If you go left, *turn to page 113.*

If you go right, *turn to page 33.*

You stumble off after the golem, trying not to get knocked over by each of his heavy foot falls.

"Hey, where are you going?" you ask him. It actually comes out as "BrugraaAAAaaaahhh." But the golem understands your zombie talk.

The golem doesn't stop walking as he answers your question. "You want to go home, right?"

"Yeah, of course," you say. "That's why I'm here."

"Well, that's where we're going," the golem growled in his earth-moving voice.

"Um," you say. "I don't know if it was clear, but my home isn't just somewhere around the corner or something. I don't like live over there. I live in a *different world*. And not just a different *Minecraft* world, I live totally outside of the game altogether."

The golem stops and looks over his shoulder. He raises one eyebrow at you. "Game?" he says. "Minecraft?"

You realize your mistake. "Sorry, forget that. I just mean it's not a world like this one... Things aren't so... blocky?"

The golem blinks. His eyelids make the sound of a miner swinging his pickaxe. "Don't fret, little green one. *I* understand. There may not be many in this... blocky... world that understand you or where you're from, but I am one." And with that, the golem decides the conversation is over and turns and keeps walking.

You notice the long vines that seem to hang from the golem's feet, dragging behind him with each step. His feet are also totally covered in moss. It almost looks like he's wearing shoes.

You desperately want to ask how all that happened, but he didn't take the last question very well...

If you ask the golem about his feet, *turn to page 25.*

If you just keep quiet, *turn to page 29.*

Your feet stay firmly planted to the spot.

You watch as the giant stone golem marches out of the ruins that you found him in and disappears into the fog that seems to have fallen all around you.

Sure, maybe this golem knows everything about this world. Sure, maybe it's been standing here since the world began. Maybe it knows everything about everything. About strange prophecies and Chosen Ones and how worlds begin, but what he doesn't know about… is you.

And *you* know you.

And you know that you're not some "Chosen One" or "hero". You're just some scared kid who wants to wake up from this dream and go home to your house and your bed and your family.

If that golem is looking for a hero, he'll have to look somewhere else, because you aren't the one who will be doing the saving, you are the one that *needs* saving.

You look around for the companion that you'd come here with. The fog is thick now.

Wait, you think, *is there even fog in Minecraft? Like sometimes it's at the very edge of the loaded area, but it shouldn't be this close. This is a strange place.*

You call out for your companion, but they're nowhere around. They must have scampered off after you began talking to the golem. That is too bad, because you have no idea where you are.

Alright, you think to yourself, *you can get out of this. Just find a cave or something to wait out the day and then you can work on making it home after that.* You swallow hard. *Wherever home is…*

You choose a direction by spinning around with one arm pointing out. When you teeter to a stop, you start walking in the direction you're pointing.

It's hard to walk in a straight line here, there are two many obstacles in these ruins. You have to keep making detours around old, broken buildings, and you can never be sure if you're walking in the same direction afterwards. For all you know, you could be going in circles!

These ruins seem to go on forever. It must have been hours, and still you're walking in these ruins. They definitely weren't that big when you walked into them. At least they didn't look that big…

You stop. Your poor, rotting feet are tired. This place looks exactly the same as everywhere else you've been tonight. It looks exactly the same as where you started. Even that broken building over there has exactly the same shape as that one the golem was standing in front of…

The ground is starting to vibrate. It's been doing that for a little while, but now it's getting harder. Regular, like clockwork, the ground shakes.

And then you hear a familiar, but mysterious noise, a voice that sounds like two stones being rubbed together. "It's a shame the Chosen One left," the voice says through the fog. It seems to be coming from everywhere at once. "It's time to return to my place and wait again."

The golem? What is it doing here? And what did it mean 'return to my place'?

You see something big looming in the air above you in the fog. It is massive and stony and all at once it comes down on top of you.

CRUNCH.

The golem steps down and doesn't even notice your little zombie body beneath his foot.

"I wonder where the Chosen One went," he wonders to himself.

THE END

To go back to the last choice and try again, *turn to page 6*. Or flip to the beginning and choose a new story!

Maybe it's because this giant stone guy is the best chance you've had so far at going home, or maybe it is because you have a hundred more questions for him, or maybe it is because, just a little bit, you *want* to be the Chosen One. But whatever the reason, you follow him.

He spins his head all the way around again, like a really creepy, giant, grey owl. He looks down at you.

"Good," says the golem. "You've made the right choice. That's exactly what the Chosen One would do."

You swallow. "So all this Chosen One stuff…" you say. "I know you said something about a prophecy. What's that all about?"

"Hmmm," says the golem. "You wish to know the prophecy?"

"Yeah, I mean, I figure it's about me— I mean, the Chosen One, so I figure I should know about it," you say.

"Perhaps, perhaps," the golem said, but didn't say anything else.

You are walking through the strange fog that had descended all around you, moving as fast as your squat little zombie legs can take you, trying to keep up with the massive strides of the golem.

"Well, once, long ago," the golem starts.

You brighten up, you didn't think that you were going to hear anything.

"There was someone just like you," the golem continues. "He came to this server as a player, but one day, he awoke in the body of a mob, just like you. He did many things, many great things, things that make sure that this server is still standing here today. Without him…" the golem trailed off.

"Yes?" you say.

The golem coughs. It sounds like an explosion. "Anyways, after he came, he found a way to get home, to leave this place. But before he did, a witch made a prophecy. She said… at a certain time, someone would come again, just like him, to… well… anyways."

It's clear that he's not saying something.

The golem starts marching towards a village that sits at the top of a nearby hill.

If you ask the golem about the prophecy, *turn to page 85.*

If you follow along silently, *turn to page 20.*

"Hey, I've got another question, big stone man," you say.

The golem just stares forward, apparently transfixed by the pool of lava in front of him.

You walk up to him and tap him on the foot. "Hey, golem guy, I need your help. I've got no idea how to find all those things you just said. You can't just leave me like this," you say.

The golem does exactly nothing.

"Okay, this is getting old," you say. "The silent treatment, really?"

But the silent treatment just continues.

You're getting annoyed now.

"HELLO!?" you shout. "CAN YOU HEAR ME!?"

If he can, the golem doesn't make any sign of it.

With your stubby little zombie arms you crawl up onto his foot and then up his leg. You hook your hands over his shoulder and pull yourself up next to his ear.

"I! NEED! YOUR! HELP!" you scream, as loud as you can.

This, finally, seems to get to him. He stirs. He moves his head slightly. He opens his mouth to speak.

Finally, you think. *Let's get some help here.*

"The Chosen One will know what to do," he says, at long last.

"What?" you say, shocked.

His lips close and again, he is perfectly still.

"That's it!" You're really annoyed now.

You climb down from the golem and look up at him with a grimace on your face.

"Well…" you say, just to yourself. "I have no *idea* what to do. But… I guess I could just make it up?"

If you go to the surface and pretend to know what to do, *turn to page 57*.

If you give up, *turn to page 56*.

"Golem!" you shout. "Elder Golem!"

Now that you've done it, you realize just how silly it is. There's *no way* that the golem can hear you, right?

You stare at your feet, deciding what to do. If you try to go back to the beginning and bring him with you, will you be able to find your way back? Heck, will you be able to find your way out in the first place?

Your train of thought is interrupted by a low rumbling that fills the room.

What's that?

Another crash sounds comes far away and the floor shakes again. It's like a very sudden, violent earthquake!

Earthquakes don't exist in Minecraft, do they?

CRASH! Another loud noise resonates through the room. It seems to be getting louder... closer...

And then the door behind you explodes. You dive for the floor, covering your head with your hands. As the dust settles, you roll over and look up.

It's the golem, standing nonchalantly in the giant hole where the door used to be.

"Little green one," the golem says. "Good to see you again."

"Hey..." you say. You're still a little stunned from his sudden appearance.

"This is it," he says. "This is what we need. Well done."

You stare up at the staircase, the weird circle of stones and the lava beneath it.

"*This* is what we need?" you ask.

"Yes," the golem says slowly. "Do you know what you've found?"

"A really terrible hot tub and the worst diving board ever?" you say sarcastically.

This seems to catch the golem off-guard. He looks at the stairs and the pool of lava below.

"Well... no," the golem says very seriously, which makes you laugh.

"This is an End portal," he says.

Your brain starts whirring. You've heard about this before. The End portal takes you to "The End" another realm in the world of Minecraft. It's a place full of Endermen and even the Ender Dragon! You realize that the golem might have made a mistake…

"Oh no," you say. "I don't live in the End. When I said I was from a different world, I didn't mean there. It's outside of the End or any world you've ever heard of. How do I explain it—"

The golem stamps its foot suddenly and your mouth snaps shut.

"No," the golem says solemnly. "I know. Of course you don't come from the End. But the End has something that you need…"

"What?" you ask.

"When the last one like you went home… he started here. The portal back to your world. It's through there. It's in the End." The golem points to the circle of stone.

"Oh," you say, swallowing. "Okay, then I should go through." You take a couple quick steps up the stairs.

"Stop!" the golem says quickly. "It's not ready. If you go through now, you will just be burnt. The portal is not activated yet. To do that, you must bring together the *light* and the *dark*."

"The light and the dark?" You're tired of the golem's mysterious way of talking. "What do you mean?"

"Only in the union of the light and the dark will you be able see through to the other—"

"No!" you interrupt. "What do I actually have to *do*?"

The golem clears his throat. He looks a bit annoyed. "A blaze rod and an ender pearl, you must bring them together."

"That's not so hard—" you start.

"*Twelve* times. Twelve of each will open the portal," the golem says and then settles down into his spot in the doorway.

"Oooohhh," you say. "That's not so easy." You tap your foot on the ground a couple times. "So where do we go next?"

The golem doesn't move or say anything.

"Hello?" you say.

"There is no 'we', only 'you' now, Chosen One," the golem says and then freezes again, as still as a stature.

You stare up at the big, grey creature, and then look around the room that you're in.

Well you're not going to find either of the things you're looking for *here*.

If you go back to the surface, *turn to page 57*.

If you pester the golem for more help, *turn to page 14*.

Endermen don't seem to care too much about looks. You'll just make them a dirt house and they won't even notice.

First up, you gotta dig some dirt.

Without a shovel or even a pickaxe, you point your fist at the ground and strike hard. Your hand kind of sinks into the dirt.

That's… weird?

You try it again and your hand just mushes into the ground. It's like trying to dig a hole with a shovel made of Nerf.

What's going on?!

You look at your hand. You know… there is something weird. Your hand's green…

OF COURSE!

Zombies can't dig! Zombies can't build! Zombie hands can't do anything! How could you have forgotten?

"Having trouble over there?" The enderman's raspy voice surprises you. You turn around in a hurry.

"Uh… no, no!" you say. "Everything's good."

"Mmmhmm," the enderman says, unimpressed.

You turn around and half-heartedly try digging at the ground. Your brain is spinning.

"That doesn't look like it's working," a suddenly loud voice says.

You spin around. The whole huddle of enderman is *right behind you!*

"AHH!" you say, jumping back.

"Can you build us a house?" one enderman demands. "Can you?! YOU PROMISED!"

"I didn't promise!" you stammer.

"You said you would! That's a promise!" the enderman shouts. His eyes are turning red. So are the eyes of the dark huddle behind him.

You don't know what to say. You just stare.

"DON'T LOOK AT ME!" the enderman hisses.

"Oh, sorry." You stare at the ground.

"Can you or can you not build us a house— LOOK AT ME WHEN I'M TALKING TO YOU." The enderman is shaking mad now.

You glance up again, confused. "Well, I thought I could, but I forgot that, well… it's hard to explain."

"STOP LOOKING AT ME!" the enderman rages.

And just like that you are charged by twenty-three angry, homeless endermen. That's about as bad as it can get.

THE END

To go back a couple choices and try again, *turn to page 70.*

To go back to the moment you returned to the surface and choose a new direction, *turn to page 57.*

Or, flip to the beginning and try again!

Maybe it's best just to keep your mouth shut. This golem doesn't seem like the sort of guy who is easily convinced of anything. If he has made up his mind not to tell you any more, maybe there is a reason.

You slot the 'prophecy' tidbit away in your brain for later. You'll probably need that at some point. But for now, you just focus on sticking close to the golem and keeping your eyes open.

The golem keeps going full speed ahead right into the village. Villagers start pouring out of their houses as the golem approaches. They are screaming and running out the town. You watch their long, silly noses flop up and down as they run in their long robes. What funny looking creatures.

The golem doesn't even seem to notice them as he walks right up to the well in the centre of the town. With all your attention focused on the golem, you notice something small. He's looking around for something around the well. Finally he stops and raises a fist.

What is it? You crane your neck to see what it was he was looking for. Beneath him you notice something strange. Instead of the cobbled path and gardens that normally fill the ground in the village, beneath the golem there is a five-block-by-five-block square of dirt that is so over grown in grass and flowers that you almost didn't notice it.

It's like there was a hole here before. Maybe the golem is returning to a place that he's already dug before.

You decide to ask. "Have you been here before?" you say as he pounds his massive fist into the ground, totally obliterating the five-block-by-five-block area.

The golem glances at you. "I have, once, long before. You're quite observant…"

You try not to smile too obviously.

The golem drills down into the earth. He seems to want you to follow him, so you hop down after. When you get to the bottom of the hole, you notice a neat little door in the side of the hole that enters some sort of underground tunnel. The golem gestures you inside and you walk in.

It's not just some cavern or cave. You find yourself in a perfectly rectangular room, well carved and medieval styled. It's gloomy here and you here the far away noise of zombie groans. It strikes fear into your heart until you realize, that that's what you sound like too…

"Where do we go now?" You groan at the golem, staring at the two doors in front of you.

"We're looking for a room with a pool of lava," the elder golem says. "I can't fit through the doors, you must find it and I will follow you once you've found it."

You nod and take a step forward.

If you go through the door on the right, *turn to page 8*.

If you go through the door on the left, *turn to page 23*.

With your mind racing, you open the door and slip through, closing it behind you. This room is square.

No lava yet, you remind yourself, trying to keep your mind on the goal.

You stumble across the floor to one of the other three doors in the room. Just as you're about to go through this one, you look back. You have to remember which way you came from, in case you need to go back.

You squint at the three other doors in the room. They all look the same. *Which one, which one?*

You race back across the room and yank the door open. A grey room stands on the other side.

No, no, that wasn't it.

You close that door and try another.

Behind that door is small stone room. *Is this one it?* It's hard to remember where you came from.

You just choose the next door and plow through it. *This has to be it.* But this room has four doors. *Is this where you came from?*

Your mind spins as you open door after door, trying to find where you came from. Before too long, you collapse onto a low stone block.

Admit it, you're lost.

You look forlornly at the identical wooden doors that spread out before you.

There's no way to get back. There's no use in going forward. You'll be lost in this maze forever…

THE END

If you want to go back to the room with five doors and try again, *turn to page 72. Or flip to the beginning and choose a new story!*

You push the door open a crack and don't see any giant zombie-eating monsters or a giant pit or pool of lava, so you figure it's safe to go all the way in. The sight of rows of bookshelves meets you. Books cover all the walls and fill the entire room. There's hardly room to move around the bookshelves.

You look up and see a balcony above you that goes all the way around the outside of the room. In the centre of the ceiling, a wooden chandelier hangs, topped with a couple burning torches.

Wood doesn't seem like the best material for a chandelier… you think.

You wander around the outside of the room and find a ladder that leads up to the balcony. There's no other exit down here, so you climb up it. There are more books up here. All the walls are covered in them. Well *almost* all the walls. There's a door down in one corner and in another corner there is a chest with something above it on the wall. It looks like a piece of paper or something. *A little strange…*

You walk to the corner and put your hand on the doorknob.

If you go through the door, *turn to page 72.*

If you go examine the paper on the wall, *turn to page 79.*

"Alright jellies," you shout. "Want a piece of me? Then you can have it!"

Wait, that doesn't sound that good. That sounds like I'm going to lose, you think. But then one of the jellies leaps right at you. It's green poisonous flesh touches you and you leap back, your skin stinging.

"Ow!"

You go to swing at this jelly. "Hiya!" Your green fist sinks into it's big green side. All the skin on your hand starts to burn.

"Aaagh!" you jump back. "That was a terrible idea."

You scramble around for a weapon of some sort until you realize that you don't have anything on you.

Uh oh.

The jellies get closer and closer. Another leaps at you and your whole left side explodes in pain.

You're backed up against the wall now. You can't fight them. You can't run. You should have taken your chance when you had it.

For a moment, everything is still and then the biggest of the jellies leaps at you and absorbs your whole face into it.

You explode into a pile of rotting flesh.

Each jelly sucks up a piece of it and slowly migrates back to their own little corners. In a way, they *did* get a piece of you…

THE END

To go back to the last choice and try again, *turn to page 47.* Or *flip to the beginning and choose a new story!*

"Hey, Mr. Golem?" you say, with a little tremble in your voice.

The golem's foot smacks into the ground and sets off a shockwave so strong that it knocks over two oak trees nearby. He grinds to a halt.

"What?" he asks. Somehow the single word takes forever to come out of his slow, stony mouth, but also sounds short and snippish.

"Oh just a question." You're already regretting opening your mouth.

The golems twin boulders of mossy eyebrows rise as he looks at you.

"Okay, I was just looking at your feet and I noticed all the green stuff dangling from them and covering them. How did that… happen?" You swallow quickly as you realize how easy it would be for him to step on you.

The golem's big head droop down to look at his feet.

"I suppose I haven't done much walking lately," the golem mumbles. "I've been waiting, watching, standing in that same place. This is the farthest away I've been from home in many years."

"You've just been standing there? In that one place where I found you?" you ask, flabbergasted.

"I suppose, yes," the golem says thoughtfully. "There hasn't been much reason to move. Not when I was just waiting…"

"Waiting for what?" you ask quickly.

"You," the golem says simply.

You miss a step and almost fall on your face. "It's hard to get used to that," you say under your breath. "So, how long have you been there anyway? A couple days?"

The golem turns and raises his eyebrows again.

"Weeks?" you try again.

He blinks.

"Since the beginning," he said. "Years, for sure. Many years."

"The beginning?" you ask. "Of this world?"

"Yes."

"When's the last time you moved?" you ask.

The golem thinks for a second. "When I sent the last one home."

"The last one?" you repeat dumbly.

"Yes, the last one like you, at the very beginning of this world. And when we sent him home, there was a prophecy that there'd be another, and so I waited."

The golem takes another couple steps while you try to process it all.

"And here we are," the golem adds.

He has quite a lead at this point and you scamper after him as fast as your little zombie legs can scamper. You don't want to get left alone in the fog.

Your mind is boiling with questions, but you're distracted as you hear screams and shouts ahead of you. There are buildings emerging from the mist... it looks like a village!

But the villagers are scattering in every direction. They apparently aren't too fond of a giant stone golem marching into the middle of their town.

And for good reason: In the smack middle of the town, the golem stops at the well and smashes one of his big fists into the ground. Dirt and rock go flying everywhere. After a couple more swings, and a spray of blocks, the golem has dug a hole that goes pretty far into the ground. You hop down into the hole after him.

"I *definitely* don't live here," you quip, but the golem just ignores.

He swings his fist again and more stone flies. But this time, something's different. There's a gap in the wall of the hole. There's a cavern or something down here. With the careful swipe of a finger, the golem makes a hole big enough to go through and then stoops and walks through the hole he's created into the mysterious cavern.

You follow.

Inside, there's a curious, square chamber. It's been well mined and has a sort of medieval style to it. You recognize this from somewhere. You've been in a place like this before, as a player... it's a stronghold.

As your eyes get used to the gloom you notice something else in the room: two doors.

"I'm too big to fit through," the golem explains. "We are looking for the room with a pool of lava. You must go looking for it and I'll follow you."

You nod dutifully and look at the doors.

If you go through the door on the right, *turn to page 8*.

If you go through the door on the left, *turn to page 23*.

This door opens up into a dingy room. Well, it's more of a hallway, really. Along the right side of the room are a series of bars that run from the floor to the ceiling. Behind the bars are several small jail cells.

But there is something more interesting about this hallway. It's the *noise*.

A gut-wrenching clanging fills the hallway and your ears. After a second of listening carefully, you notice that the noise is coming from down the hall. It's echoing from the very end of the hall. It sounds metallic, rough, violent and just a little wet.

What's down there?

To satisfy your curiosity, you start walking towards the noise. Each time the clang fills the hallway, you flinch. It's not your fault, you can't help it.

Another couple steps and your left hand, which is dragging along the left wall, falls on something that isn't stone. You look to your left and see a door set into the wall here. You kind of want to go through it, but not before you figure out where *the noise* is coming from.

You take a deep breath, steel your nerves, and keep going. There are only five cells left. *Four. Three. Two.*

You peek around the stone dividing wall. All you see is an empty cell at the end of the row, drenched in shadows. Everything inside is just... black.

And then something black jumps from our of the blackness. A spider launches itself right at your face.

"Aaaaaaaiiiieee!" you scream like your mom in the scary part of *any* movie, even the not-so-scary ones.

But the spider smashes against the iron bars, unable to reach you. It jumps back to the back of the cell and hurls itself forward again. The sickening, wet clang echoes in your ears.

If you free the spider, *turn to page 73*.

If you go through the door, *turn to page 66*.

If you go back to the room with five doors, *turn to page 72*.

You bite your tongue. Or at least you try to, but when you do, you realize that you don't even have a tongue. You hadn't noticed it until right now. Now you can't stop thinking about it. It feels *so weird!*

The golem keeps walking and you keep following. Your eyes keep drifting to the vines trailing from his feet. You want to ask him *so bad.* But also, an angry giant man made of stone does not sound like a boatload of fun. With all your self control, you manage to keep your mouth firmly closed.

A couple minutes later, the golem stops. You look around, you don't seem to be anywhere in particular… There are a couple trees nearby but mostly just a couple small hills and a whole bunch of grass. You thought that your mysterious destination was going to be a *lot* more exciting than this.

You look back up to notice the golem staring you down.

"What?" you ask, wondering if you have got something on your face. Maybe some brains…

"Were you going to say something?" the golem asked slowly, each word rolling off of its granite lips.

You shake your head defensively. "No, no."

The golem gives you a look and then keeps walking. But you notice from time to time now he looks back over his shoulder.

What was that, you wonder. *Was he trying to catch you in a trap? Get you to ask something so he could blast you? No, you are too smart for that.*

The golem marches into the centre of a village, sending the villagers scattering.

"Sorry," you say to any of them that pass. "Sorry about him, you know he gets into one of his moods and then just has to march into villages all *clomp, clomp, clomp.* Sorry. You know, he's nice once you get to know him."

They just scream and run.

"Kinda," you add under your breath.

Right beside the well, the golem stoops down and with the blow of a fist, bashes a chunk of rock out of the ground.

Your eyebrows rise so high they almost climb into your hairline, but you keep your mouth firmly closed.

The golem looks at you and cocks his head to the side. You just shrug your shoulders and try to look uninterested.

And if that isn't weird enough, the golem climbs out of the hole and starts to do a weird little dance in circles around the well in the centre of the village.

Maybe this guy is off his rocker, you think. You giggle a little to yourself about using the word *rock*er. Get it?

Maybe he's lost his marbles! You're pretty proud of the marble pun. (It's a type of rock.)

You look up and realize that all this time, the golem has been staring at you.

"What?" he growls. "Nothing?"

You don't know what to say.

"You don't have any questions about any of this?" the golem says.

You try to open your mouth, but he just keeps plowing forward.

"I know you're not the real Chosen One. You can't be. This is very sad, I was excited that the Chosen One had finally arrived. But you're just some other weird zombie. The Chosen One is curious, full of questions. The Chosen One would ask about all of this! The vines on my feet and the village and the hole we're digging. But you, you don't even care. I'm sorry," he says. "I can't take you home."

And then, just like that, the golem marches out of town.

You try to follow him, you try to explain, but as you do he just shouts back at you.

"Don't follow me! If you do, I'll step on you!"

He disappears off into the fog. You stay stuck in place.

After a while, the villagers start creeping back into the town. They all gather in a crowd behind a building and then all at once they rush out at you, driving you from the village.

You run, lost in this strange world, all alone.

THE END

To go back to the last choice and try again, *turn to page 9. Or flip to the beginning and choose a new story!*

It's best to check it out first… *what could go wrong?*

You take a couple steps up the staircase and notice that there is something embedded in them, half way up. It's a little cage, filled with silverfish. Those tiny, nasty little monsters that fill dungeons sometimes.

You're a zombie though, remember? Nothing to worry about…

As you step closer, the silverfish start swarming out of their cage.

"'Allo, 'allo, 'allo," one says in a funny, high-pitched voice. "What are you doing here, mate?"

It takes you by surprise. "Um, I'm just taking a look," you say.

"A look, eh? A look?" another one says loudly, whizzing underneath your feet. "Whatcha wanting with a look then, mate?"

"Uh, just looking. Curious," you say, trying to keep your balance as the silverfish dart under your feet.

"Now Bernie," one silverfish says to another. "It's not like a zombie to be curious, now, is it?"

"Not really, Chad, I've never seen it and I've been around the bock once or twice or a 'undred times," the other one responds.

There are six of them now, swarming under your feet.

You're starting to get sweaty and nervous.

"I thought this might be a way to get home—" you try to explain.

"'Ome?!" another silverfish exclaims. "I've never known a zombie with an 'ome!"

"Well, I'm not a zombie," you say defensively. "I'm a player, in this body, and I'm trying to get home!"

"Player! Player! Player!" the silverfish start screaming and tons of them start pouring out of the cage now.

"No, ah, stop!" you shout as they get under your feet and start pushing you. You lose your balance and tumble over.

You're right on the edge of the stairs though. The only place to fall is… off of them. You try to catch the stone as you go down, but your slow zombie hand misses. And you tumble past the staircase into the lava pool below.

Tsssssssssss.

Scorched zombie smells terrible.

THE END

To go back to the last choice and try again, *turn to page 3. Or flip to the beginning and choose a new story!*

You cautiously enter this new room. It's huge.

Only a couple torches on the wall throw light around this massive room leaving many dark spots. Your zombie eyes peer into those spots and see just a couple piles of bones and some arrows.

Maybe something happened here recently…

Things are mostly quiet here but once in a while, a groan echoes through the room bouncing off every wall. As you wander to the right in this room, those occasional groans get louder, before they stop all together. You have found two doors in your exploration of this room. One's on the left wall, one's on the right.

If you take the left door, *turn to page 113*.

If you take the right door, *turn to page 72*.

"Okay," you say. "I'm sorry, really sorry for not telling you sooner. You were only helpful and kind to me, you deserved the truth. I should have told you, I'm sorry. I was only scared you wouldn't help me if I did."

She nods. "I understand, it's okay."

"And," you say. "I *promise*, I won't eat a single person! That's not my thing anyways."

She smiles. "Good. I believe you. Don't break that trust."

She reaches out for your hand and drags you into the cottage.

Garbanzo is sitting behind a desk which is covered in emeralds and gold and brown bags of other treasures. As he sees you, he grabs these things and pull them closer to him.

"Alright Garbanzo," the old lady says. "Don't worry about this guy. He may be a zombie, but he's a nice zombie. Wouldn't hurt a fly—"

"I'm not worried about flies…" Garbanzo remarks worriedly.

"Be nice!" Madame Mole snaps. "My friend here wants to buy something from you."

"A zombie wants to buy something?" Garbanzo says in disbelief.

"Yes," she answers. "He needs twelve ender pearls. You have them right?"

Garbanzo looks suspicious. "Yes…" He grabs a bag from under the desk and smacks it down on top. "But it will cost you. Can the zombie pay?"

"Yes," the woman says, "of course. Right?"

She turns to you.

If you say that you can pay, *turn to page 59.*

If you grab the pearls, *turn to page 114.*

With your mind racing, you open the door and slip through, closing it behind you. This room is square.

No lava yet, you remind yourself, trying to keep your mind on the goal.

You stumble across the floor to one of the other three doors in the room. Just as you're about to go through this one, you look back. You have to remember which way you came from, in case you need to go back.

You squint at the three other doors in the room. They all look the same. *Which one, which one?*

You race back across the room and yank the door open. A grey room stands on the other side.

No, no, that wasn't it.

You close that door and try another.

Behind that door is small stone room. *Is this one it?* It's hard to remember where you came from.

You just choose the next door and plow through it. *This has to be it.* But this room has four doors. *Is this where you came from?*

Your mind spins as you open door after door, trying to find where you came from. Before too long, you collapse onto a low stone block.

Admit it, you're lost.

You look forlornly at the identical wooden doors that spread out before you. There's no way to get back. There's no use in going forward. You'll be lost in this maze forever…

THE END

If you want to go back to the room with five doors and try again, *turn to page 72.* Or *flip to the beginning and choose a new story!*

"Oh… uh, n-n-no reason," you stutter. "Just, like, curious."

The blind lady raises her eyebrows sceptically. "Oh," she says. "You do know that they're very dangerous and easily angered creatures. It's not a good idea to just go looking for them."

"I'm not… worried," you say.

"You're a strange duck," the lady says.

"I'm not a duck," you say without thinking. And then you immediately regret it. *Why'd I say that? Of course I'm not a duck…*

"Oh, well then what are you?" the old lady asks with just the corner of a smile. Clearly she's joking. But you start panicking.

"Nothing special, the same thing everyone is. Of course. Ha ha ha ha." Your fake laughs are very obviously fake.

The old lady is starting to get suspicious. "No, what are you? You have to pardon an old lady who can't see. I know it's a rude question. But if I could see you, I wouldn't need to ask."

"I'm, just, I'm like you. I'm a player—" you say without thinking.

"A *player?*" the old lady asks loudly.

"No, no, no. Ha ha, just a mistake, I'm a villager. Right, we're all villagers!" you say.

"Then why'd you say you were a player?" the old lady asks.

"A joke?" you try.

"Well, anyways," she says. "You're clearly not a player. No player talks like you. They all TALK LIKE THIS!"

You smile. *True.*

"But I don't think you're a villager either… For one thing, you're not from this village are you?" The woman pokes her finger into your chest.

"No," you say quickly. "Of course not."

"Well, that's strange, because most villagers never stray too far out of their own village, now that I think about it." She pokes you again.

You can feel yourself sweating cube-shaped drops of sweat.

"Oh well, I'm… weird," you say. It's all you can think of.

"Sure are," she retorts. And then sticks her fingers in her mouth and whistles.

"Help! Help!" she yells.

The villagers that ran off turn around and come running back. They start circling you. One pulls out a hoe, another a shovel.

You look for a way to escape, but they are all around you.

"Get away from that zombie, Madame Mole!" one of them yells.

"Zombie?" she says, scared, confused. The villagers pull her away and then all leap at you at once with their gardening implements.

Smack, smack, smack!

THE END

To go back to the last choice and try again, *turn to page 52.*

To go back to the moment you returned to the surface and choose a new direction, *turn to page 57.*

Or, *flip to the beginning and choose a new story!*

Who knows where to find a couple dozen creepers at this hour? Maybe these villagers will have an idea!

You lurch over towards the huddle of villagers.

As you get close, they spot you and start screaming and running with their hands above their heads and their noses flopping with every step. It's complete chaos!

Only one of the villagers doesn't run off. She looks very old and is just staring dumbly at the wall of a nearby house. *What's up with her?*

If you follow the fleeing villagers, *turn to page 81.*

If you approach the old lady, *turn to page 82.*

"That would be great!" you say. "I'd never thought of getting ender pearls that way!" *Thank goodness you talked to this woman, she's smart!*

The old villager smiles and reaches out for your arm. "I'm going to need you to help me, guide me. With my vision the way it is, I'm not the best at exploring the wilds by myself…"

You feel a little bit worried as she grabs hold of your arm but you let her. As she gets close she sniffs a little.

Of course, you think. *When you lose one of your senses your other senses get stronger. She's going to be able to tell I'm a zombie!*

"Hmm," she says, leaning in closer. "You need some deodorant. Alright off we go! Which way's the sun?"

Phew, you dodged a bullet.

You squint up at the clouds, trying to keep the rain from falling right in your eyes.

You see the sun trying to hide behind an angry grey cloud.

"Over there!" you say, pointing

She makes an unimpressed face.

"Oh right, sorry," you say timidly. "This way." You turn yourself and her to face the sun.

"Good, it's the evening, so that's the west, which means…" The old lady spins quickly around. "We're going this way. Step to it!"

Together you tromp through the rain. The sun sinks lower and lower in the sky until it is sitting right on the horizon, lighting up the grey clouds in oranges and dark purples. And then it is gone all together.

But that doesn't stop you guys. You can see in the dark and she doesn't need light anyways.

Before long, little twinkles of light can be seen on the horizon. A couple minutes later you see they are coming from the village ahead. Furnaces and torches blaze in the little houses, lighting them up.

The old lady sniffs. "We're here," she says. She directs you to a house at the outskirts of the town and then raps heavily on the door.

A minute later, the door is thrown open. A villager stands on the other side, wearing a purple robe, his hands hidden in his sleeves. He grumbles loudly about the time of night and the rain and 'who would be visiting at this hour!'

But the minute that he stares out at the two of you he screams and slams the door. The scream is *very* high-pitched. Like when a lady in a cartoon sees a mouse.

"Well, that's rude of him," the old lady says. "Garbanzo is a grumpy old man, but he's usually not *that* bad."

You think you have an idea about why he might be being so rude…

She knocks again and you notice that the man, Garbanzo, is watching you from the window of his house. Slowly, hesitantly, he creeps to the door and opens it a crack.

"Madame Mole," he whispers. "Are you okay? Blink once for yes, twice for no."

The old lady, who's apparently named Madame Mole, has a face that makes it clear that she thinks Garbanzo is being *pretty* dumb. "No," she says testily. "I'm fine, now stop acting like a crazy. We need to buy something."

"But you're with a— a—" Garbanzo is stuttering at the word.

If you let him reveal you're a zombie, *turn to page 51*.

If you interrupt him, *turn to page 42*.

She's going to very quickly realize that we're not actually old friends, you realize as you stand slowly.

You drag your feet as you walk hesitantly towards the small huddle of the old lady and endermen. They're all standing close, listening to the things that she said. *She was right, they do seem to have taken a liking to her.*

And then you have an idea: *Probably because she can't look at them! She can't make them mad! She's the perfect friend for some endermen!*

You drag your feet right up to the old woman, and join the strange little huddle of endermen, staring at everyone's feet.

"Look!" she says to the endermen, "Look who I brought you!"

The endermen all look over at you. You glance up at them, trying to figure out how they are going to react. You remember Fibula saying something about how they don't mind so much if a fellow mob looks at them. They still don't seem to love it. You quickly look back down again.

One of the endermen hisses and rasps at the old lady. "Who is it?" they ask.

She smiles, but her eyebrows twist into an expression of confusion. "Your long lost friend—" she says, stopping and turning to you. "Actually, I didn't get your name, sorry dear."

Everyone's watching you, waiting for your response. You clear your throat and say, "Rotney, my name's Rotney."

"Weird name," the old lady says. "But pretty, very pretty." She's trying to be nice.

The endermen, on the other hand, are just staring at you, more than a little confused. Of course, they don't recognize you.

The old lady is getting antsy. "Rotney, aren't you happy to be back with your friends?"

Everyone's waiting for your response. Your cover is going to get blown any second. You need to make a plan.

If you tell the old lady the truth, *turn to page 110.*

If you signal to the endermen to play along, *turn to page 67.*

"A paying customer?" you ask, cutting the merchant off. You hoped that this would shut him up, but instead it makes him scream. Not at all the reaction that you were looking for…

What you didn't count on, is that your scolding words just came out as a terrible growl.

"*Aiee!*" he screams backing away from the door.

"Well, I'm so sorry," the old lady says, turning to you. "Garbanzo is just being incredibly rude right now. Imagine, making fun of someone because of the way they talk! Here let me go in and talk some sense into him."

If she goes in there, you think, *then he'll tell her what I really am. I can't let that…*

You grab her arm, stopping her from going in.

"What?" she says, clearly shocked.

"Don't go in there," you say quietly. "If he's going to act like that, then I don't want to do business with him anyways."

"But…" the old lady says. "What about the ender pearls. You needed them so bad. Let me go get them for you…"

"No!" you say. "No, I don't need them that bad, it's fine."

"Okay," she says. "Well then, what's next? I guess I can't help you anymore."

You bite your lip. "I guess not."

"Well… then…" she says, "do you need a place to stay for the night?"

"Oh, no!" you say, a little too forcefully.

"Okay… then, bye?" she says.

You blink. "Yeah, I guess so."

You wander off into the night, a little lost. You missed your chance. She was the one who could help you. Now, you don't know where you are and you don't have any ender pearls.

You wander off into the night, hopeless and lost. And starting to hate being a zombie…

THE END

To go back a couple choices and try again, *turn to page 39.*

To go back to the moment you returned to the surface and choose a new direction, *turn to page 57.*

Or, flip to the beginning and choose a new story!

You head towards the top of the hill.

The swamp turns into a lovely grassy hill. You can't see the top of the hill yet through the fog. But as you get a little higher the fog starts to break away.

What are you expecting to find at the top of this hill, you ask yourself. *It's not like there are going to be twelve endermen just huddled at the very top…*

You shake your head, feeling a little dumb. And then the fog finally clears and you can see the top of the hill.

You stop in your tracks.

Unbelievable.

You were right, there are not twelve endermen huddled at the top of the hill. There are twenty-three endermen huddled at the top of the hill.

What are the chances?

Filled with a new rush of excitement, you book it up to the top of the hill.

"Hey, hey guys," you say quickly. "Hey, I've been looking for you." You're panting for breath. You make sure not to stare directly at any of them. You hear that endermen don't like that very much…

The ground is still a little wet here, there is dew settled all over the grass, and as you run, little tubular droplets of water fly in every direction. As you stomp to a stop in front of the endermen, you spray a cascade of water towards them. They jump back and screech terrible screams. The couple in front that get hit by the dew quickly wipe off their legs with their long arms.

"Ew, gross," you hear one of them say.

"Wha- what's going on?" you ask. "Do you not like water?"

The endermen all stare at you. It's like getting caught in twenty-three sets of headlights all at once.

"Not like water?" one of them asks. "Yeah, OF COUSE! Who *would* like water?"

You stare back at them dumbly. "I don't… mind it," you say. "It's fun to play in."

"Well, *you're* weird," says the enderman.

Someone's weird here, you agree. But you don't think it's you.

You shuffle your feet a bit in the grass, sending a couple small drops flying.

The huddle of endermen shuffles back altogether.

"All endermen hate water," says the tallest enderman in the front. "It's just so wet and… weird. We've got nothing like that at home…"

Now that they say it, it starts to ring a bell. You've never seen an enderman on a beach. *At home?* That's right, the endermen come from The End, and there's no water there, is there?

You look around at all the streams and lakes around you. It's kind of a weird place for them to hang out.

If you threaten to splash them if they don't give you their pearls, *turn to page 96*.

If you ask them why they're here, *turn to page 70*.

You set off towards the massive stone arch that dominates the horizon. As you get closer, you realize that this arch is the size of a mountain. A *very big* mountain. The top of the arch actually looks quite a bit like a mountain. It has whole forests growing on top of it.

What makes it quite different than a mountain is the big hole punched out of the middle of it. Swamps and plains and lakes covered the ground that falls under the massive stone arch. Minecraft geography is weird. And its even weirder to see it with your own eyes!

It's a long walk. The arch always looks like it will be right over the next hill. But when you get over the hill, you see that there's another hill in the way. And then another hill. And another. The arch is just so huge that it always looks like it's right there.

"Are we there yet?" you whine, and then you realize there's no one around to answer. *Silly me,* you think.

"If you keep asking that, I'm going to pull these feet over right here and turn this zombie around!" you say to yourself in a deep voice and then break into giggles. That gets your spirits back up and before long, you're walking into the shadow of the giant arch. It almost blocks out the whole sky.

If you turn to your right, there is a path towards one of the two bases of the massive arch. You think you see a pretty good place to climb up onto the top of it. But, if you keep going straight, you will go right into the lands that are under it.

If you climb up the arch, *turn to page 75.*

If you go under the arch, *turn to page 109.*

This door takes you to a medium-sized room. The first thing you notice is four large jellies, one hiding in each corner. As they see you, they start to creep closer.

Quickly, your eyes scan the rest of the room. There are two torches on the wall and a couple blocks of dirt left scattered over the floor. *That's a little strange…*

There's a door on your left and another straight ahead of you.

You hear the far-off, very quiet sound of zombie moans and notice that the jellies are almost right on top of you now.

If you fight the jellies, *turn to page 24.*

If you take the door on the left, *turn to page 50.*

If you go straight, *turn to page 66.*

And if I went with you to the merchant, how am I supposed to pay for anything, you think. *Does this merchant take rotting flesh or low, angry moans as payment? 'Cause that's all I've got.*

No, that's not going to work. But you have another idea…

"Hey, you say, I actually have a question for you," you say.

"Okay?" she says. "What's up?"

"Well I was very interested in your story about meeting those strangers in the woods… I'm wondering if you've met some friends of mine…"

"Okay? What were they like? And don't tell me what they look like, because," the old woman points at her eyes, "that won't help."

"Well, they were tall. You know, their voices came from up high," you say, watching the old woman carefully.

She looks thoughtful.

"And, and," you add. "They talk very strangely, they sound a bit like this." You make a weird swallowing, crunching sound with your throat.

"Hmmm," she says.

"And sometimes they sound a bit like this." You scream at the back of your throat so you sound a bit like an underwater robot.

She shakes her head. "It does sound familiar."

"Oh! And sometimes they're very rude and just suddenly leave a conversation and run very far away very fast…" You cross your fingers.

"Oh yes! Oh yes! Very rude and confusing indeed! I remember meeting some guys just like that a couple years ago. On one of my nature walks I got separated from my guide and wandered out into the middle of nowhere. I met some people just like you've described. Very tall and they all sounded like they had a terrible cold. A *very terrible* cold. You know, I thought that they might be dangerous when I first met them. Who knows what sort of people, monsters you might meet out there. But these guys were quite nice. You know, they took a liking to me. I even learned how to understand them after a while. They lead me back to my village, but they refused to get very close. They seemed like very… private people, that's all." The woman drifted off, lost in her positive thoughts.

Perfect! Those have to be Endermen, you think.

"Wow, that's great," you say. "Would you be able to take me to them. Do you remember where they were?"

"Sure… I remember," she says. "But what about the pearls? The endermen? Isn't that more important? Getting home? What's changed so suddenly?"

She's starting to get suspicious.

You panic a little.

If you tell her she met endermen, *turn to page 83.*

If you tell her you just want to see your friends, *turn to page 98.*

This door opens not into a room, but a long corridor that winds back into the darkness.

You take a step forward and a low rumble starts. It's very quiet. Almost not there at all. It echoes down the hallway towards you.

You freeze for a second, but the rumble fades away and nothing else happens. Your eyes fix on the shadows down the hallway. There is no movement. Everything looks still, safe.

You continue down the hallway, moving slowly, watching for anything else.

Before long, you come to a door set into the side of the hallway. Your hand lingers on the doorknob. But then you notice something. Squinting through the dark, you see another door down at the end of the hallway.

Which way, you wonder.

If you take the door at the end of the hallway, *turn to page 66.*

If you take the door right beside you, *turn to page 28.*

If you go back to the room with five doors, *turn to page 72.*

"A zombie?" you say, completing Garbanzo's sentence. But to him it just sounds like hungry growls.

"A ZOMBIE!" Garbanzo screams closing the door so that there's just enough gap for one of his eyes to peer out.

The old lady turns to you. "What?! What did you say?!" She pulls her arm away from you.

You swallow. *Well, that's the end of that.*

"A zombie," you repeat. There's no use in lying now. "I'm a zombie. That's why I speak like this. That's why I smell a little bad…"

Madame Mole looks shocked, frightened.

Garbanzo throws open the door and grabs Madame Mole by the shoulders, pulling her into his shack. The door slams shut.

You stare morosely at the door. *That didn't work…*

You turn around, thinking about what to do next.

A *click* from behind startles you and you turn.

The door has opened again and Madame Mole is standing in it, her feet spread wide and her back straight.

"Friend?" she asks. "Are you still there?"

Your brain is dizzy, but you say, "Yes."

"Good, I've made a decision. We shouldn't judge you just because you're a zombie. You're a perfectly nice person. And if you'd never told me, I'd have never known. I *still* want to help you. On two conditions." She has a serious look on her face.

"Yes?" you murmur.

"One, you kept the truth from me, I don't like that. It destroys trust. I want you to apologize," she says. "And two, you have to promise you won't eat anyone. What do you say?"

If you promise and apologize, *turn to page 34*.

If you don't, *turn to page 95*.

"Hey," you say softly. "Don't freak out or anything. I have a question for you."

Her face scrunches up so that the wrinkles on her big nose looks like the surface of a stormy sea.

"You've got quite the frog in your throat," she says, after hearing your zombie moans. "Are you quite alright, child?"

You nod.

"You there?" she asks.

Oh right.

"Yes, I'm alright," you say, though you know it will just sound like moans to her.

She listens to you and then tilts her head. "That's *quite* the cold. You need sugarcane and pumpkin tea! That's what solves that every time!"

You want to tell her that she's wrong, but you know she won't understand you. *Eh, what's the harm.* You try one more time.

"No, it's not a cold," you moan. "I'm a zombie. I need your help."

She listens and then is silent.

"Hmm, maybe you haven't got a cold after all… You know, sweet young thing, you sound familiar. Back when I was just a young thing, I wandered out into the woods even though my mother said I shouldn't, not without my eyes, you know?"

You nod and then catch yourself and say "yes," instead.

"Mmhm," she says. "Well I went out there. I felt my way through the trees, listening to the pretty stories of the birds and the cheering of the grasses and the slow creaking of the old trees. And then I met several nice fellows. I'd never met them before, they'd never been through the village, and you know, they talked an awful lot like you."

What?, you think.

"I went out there everyday after that," she says. "To speak with them. And slowly I got to understand them. Or at least a bit of what they said. Sometimes they said the most *confusing* things! Like once one of them said, 'We were going to eat you, but when you weren't scared of us, we were so curious we had to get to know you better!' What a terribly curious thing to say!"

"Very curious," you say. *I guess if you can't see,* you think, *you'd never know you were talking to three zombies in the woods.*

"You'll have to forgive me, I'm quite old and my memory is shabby. But I think, if you speak, I might understand you. Try again," she insists.

Okay, let's give this a try. You open your mouth and speak slowly. "Hello, I need your help. I'm looking for some endermen."

Her face scrunches up until her nose looks like the surface of the windiest sea. Then she relaxes. "Hello to you too," she says. "I'd be happy to help you."

She really can *speak zombie!*

"But I must have misunderstood you," she says. "I thought you said you wanted to find *endermen!*"

"I did say that," you say.

Her face compresses again.

"And why would you want to do a thing like that!" she exclaims.

If you tell her about your quest, *turn to page 88.*

If you keep it a secret, *turn to page 36.*

You let the panic fill your system and you turn on your heel and move as fast as you can down the hallway, not wasting a second to look behind you.

There's no way I could beat that many zombies, you tell yourself, *especially without even a sword. Without any weapons at all!*

You run and waddle down the hallway: *SCLOMP, SCLOMP, SCLOMP, SCLOMP.* You reach the door at the other end and dash across the room to another door. You pay no attention to what direction you're going. It's your panic that is making the decisions now.

You take a right, and then a left, and pass through a room with a beautiful, golden lion statue in the middle but you don't even stop for a second to look at it. You take another right and then lose track of which directions you're taking.

In a couple minutes, your lungs are screaming and your legs are aching. You stop running. You're exhausted. You bend over at the waist, panting.

When you get your breath back, you straighten up and look around. You don't recognize this place. You don't think that you've been in this room before. It's long and skinny and lined with chests.

You open one of the chests. It's filled with fish. So is the next one. And the next one.

"This is fishy," you say, making yourself laugh. But when you hear the words come out of your mouth they just sound like *GerrrrrSCRAnnnggmm.*

After a moment of confusion, you realize your mistake: you're a zombie! You shouldn't have run! There was nothing to be scared about. Zombies don't eat other zombies…

Well, you think to yourself, *I'll just have to go back and talk to them.*

But as you go back through the door that you came through you're greeted by an unwelcome surprise.

This new room is two things: large and totally unfamiliar!

You don't remember it at all and it has about twelve doors.

There's no way that you're getting out of here.

"GOLEM!" you shout, over and over. But you hear nothing. You're totally lost, deep in the stronghold's maze. Just another zombie waiting for an unfortunate player to stumble across you...

THE END

To go back to the last choice and try again, *turn to page 92. Or flip to the beginning and choose a new story!*

"If the Chosen One would know what to do," you say to the golem, even though you know he doesn't care, "then I guess I'm not it."

The golem does nothing.

Your shoulders slump.

You didn't want to be the dumb "Chosen One" *anyways!*

You wander back through the maze feeling sorry for yourself. If only someone would come save you!

As you wander, you look up and realize you have no idea where you are! At first you were following the busted doorways that the golem had left behind. But you'd taken a wrong turn and now there was no path to follow.

You take a couple turns in a panic, searching and just find yourself in a room full of a couple creepers and a spider. They turn to look at you suspiciously and you back out of there.

You zip down a couple other corridors, hoping that you'd find a broken doorway just around the next turn.

But you never do.

With each twist and turn you only get more and more lost.

Soon, you're just another zombie in a sprawling, dark dungeon.

THE END

To go back to the last choice and try again, *turn to page 14. Or flip to the beginning and choose a new story!*

"Bye dude," you say to the golem with a little wave. He doesn't move or even notice. He might as well be a statue…

Kinda rude, you think as you sneak past him into the hallway beyond. *But at least he helped me find a chance to get back home. I guess I should just be thankful.*

You're a little worried about finding your way back through the maze until you realize that you can just follow the obvious trail of busted doorways. *Another way the golem was helpful.*

Soon enough you're back in the first room you started. You climb out of the gap in the wall into the hole that the golem dug. Rain is pouring down outside. That's good, because it looks like it's daytime. The rain will stop you from burning up immediately.

The bottom of the hole is filling slowly with rain water. The chunky dirt at your feet is getting squelchy and muddy. *Who knew Minecraft had mud?*

Even with the mud and the rain, you still manage to hop up the walls of the hole and make your way back to the surface.

The villagers are just creeping their way back into the village. They are closing doors and cleaning up after the shock of a giant stone man stomping through their homes. They just seem to be getting settled when they see you and start screaming again.

"AHHHHHHHH!"

"No, no!" you say, but of course to them it just sounds like zombie growls. *That's* not making it any better… They start running out of the village again.

These guys are just having the worst *day.*

You ignore the wandering thoughts of just how delicious those villagers would be to eat, and try to focus on the task at hand.

Blaze rods and ender pearls. Twelve of each. That's a bunch!

You know that blaze rods only come from blazes, and they only exist in the nether. The nether is another dimension, like the End, that you can only get to through a special portal. *That* was going to be a lot of work. Why not start with the easier one first?

Ender pearls were dropped by endermen, you remember. You would need to find a whole *bunch* of endermen and get them to give you all their pearls. Where to start? You look around. To your left, a crowd of villagers cower behind a nearby building. To the right a giant outcropping of rock peeks over the horizon. It's like a big natural arch. In front of you is a big lake. And behind you is the direction you came from in the first place.

If you go ask the villagers for help, *turn to page 38*.

If you start looking around the big arch, *turn to page 46*.

"Uh… yeah," you say. "Sure."

"Great," Garbanzo says, plunking the bag into your hands. "Twelve ender pearls… with the market the way it is… well… that's a lot of pearls." He does some quick calculations on a scrap of paper. "That's gonna be 67 emeralds!"

The old lady clears her throat.

"Sorry," he says, "for a friend, I can make that 60 emeralds. I'll do you a favour."

"Thanks, that's nice," you say. *But that's still 60 more emeralds that I have,* you think. The old lady translates.

Noticing the unsure look on your face, Garbanzo adds. "Well, you can pay that in gold bars instead, or… well, never mind just gold bars."

"Okay, to be honest I don't have that many emeralds or gold," you say. And after giving you a worried look, the old lady translates.

"Is there something else you'll accept?" you ask.

Madame Mole asks the man for you and his face scrunches up. "He can't pay?" he asks her. "You know, he *has* to pay."

"I know," she says. "Isn't there a way?"

He nods once. "There's a way. Is he sure he wants the pearls?"

"I'm sure. I'll pay whatever it is," you say.

Madame Mole nods and Garbanzo goes over to her and whispers something. She excuses herself from the cottage just leaving the two of you alone.

"You see," says Garbanzo opening a chest in the corner. "There's another thing that I buy quite a lot of…" He steps aside so you can see inside the chest.

Your jaw almost drops off.

"Rotten flesh!" he shouts.

The whole chest is full of it! Piles of rotten flesh!

"It's so delicious!" he drools.

Delicious! This guy's a weirdo!, you think

But in the second that you think that, Garbanzo has jumped forward with a sword in his hand. "Let me have some of yours!"

With fear coursing through your rotting brain, you turn and run. In the panic, you drop the bag of ender pearls.

You rush out the back door of the shack and into the night. And you don't stop running until you're good and far away.

How will you get back to the golem now? How will you find the pearls? You slump down onto a rock. *It's useless. I'm stuck here forever!*

THE END

To go back to the last choice and try again, *turn to page 34.*

To go back to the moment you returned to the surface and choose a new direction, *turn to page 57.*

Or, flip to the beginning and choose a new story!

This door leads to a narrow hallway on the other side that opens up into a square room with a wooden floor. It looks pretty gross and shabby in comparison to the last room. *If only every room could be made of one hundred percent gold.*

There's nothing really except some bones in the corner, and a small slime that is slowly hopping towards you. There's one other door in the room, hidden in a shadowy corner.

If you want to go back and try a different direction, *turn to page 8.*

If you want to go further into the stronghold, *turn to page 63.*

The hill is just one small location in the wetlands. You decide it's better to explore the other side.

You wade and march through the swamps and streams. You can't help but imagine how nice it would be to have a boat right now. Unfortunately, zombie hands aren't good at making anything!

You find a player cutting some reeds and you decide to keep your distance. You don't want to become some rotten flesh in his inventory. Once he's gone, you continue your adventure but don't find much of anything else, except some sheep and a little family of creepers.

You sigh. Useless.

You stare out at the curtain of rain that's falling on the far side of the arch. *Maybe they're all out there somewhere.*

If you check out the hill, *turn to page 44.*

If you head out into the land past the arch, *turn to page 80.*

You walk past the hopeful little green jelly. It's coming at you with all that it has got. But even with a slow walk, you move faster than it.

"Sorry buddy, not today," you say, waving at the jelly as you pass.

You go to the shadowy door and slip through it, careful to close it behind you so that that jelly doesn't follow you forever.

This room is similar to the last one. While the corners of the room are made of stone, there is a cross of wooden floor in the centre that extends to a door placed in the perfect centre of each of the walls of the perfectly square room.

You step onto the wooden floor and as you do, the world seems to shake and suddenly spin around you. It's like the wooden floor suddenly lifted and spun around quickly before nestling down into the stone again.

You get up from your knees, where you'd fallen and look around. *Which door is which?* There's no way to tell. Everything looks the same here.

You try to go back through the door closest to you, but when you do, it's not the same shabby room with the little jelly. No, this room looks exactly the same as the one you just left: perfectly square and with a cross of wooden floor. You accidentally stumble forward into the room, and the floor lifts again and spins you around, before finally coming to a rest. You glance nervously around the room. *Which way is which?!*

You run to a door and throw it open. It's another room exactly the same as the last two!

About twelve more times you choose a door and dash through it only to find another room exactly the same, and then get spun around.

Then, you start to give up hope. *There's no way home.* You just sit down, waiting for the floor to spin, hoping someone will find you in this terrible maze of a stronghold.

THE END

To go back to the last choice and try again, *turn to page 61. Or flip to the beginning and choose a new story!*

"Oh hey," you say casually, "you know, I could help you with that."

None of them even look away from their pearls.

"The whole mirror thing…" you continue. "My dad runs this business—"

"A zombie business?" one of the endermen interrupts.

Oh, hadn't thought of that. "Yeah," you say, trying to remain cool. "A zombie business. He's a very ambitious guy. He's eaten a… thousand brains."

The endermen all nod. They're impressed.

Phew. Dodged that bullet.

"Right, well my dad runs this business," you say. "You know, he sells mirrors. Really tall ones. You know, business isn't doing so well because they don't fit in anyone's houses—"

"And because he's a zombie," the same enderman interrupts again.

"Yeah… maybe because of that too," you say, a little annoyed. "If you guys want, I could sell you some better mirrors. I'd get you a really good price."

"We don't have any money!" one of the endermen remarks.

"Oh right," you say, pretending you hadn't thought of that yet. "You know, I really like you guys so I'll give you a real deal. If you just trade in your pearls, I'll get you a mirror each!"

There is some excited tittering among the endermen.

One steps forward. "Okay, okay, sounds good. But before I give up my pearl, I'd just like to see the mirror. I want to make sure that it's tall enough, and shiny enough!"

"Oh," you say. "I don't have them with me, but if you give me your pearls I'll be right back—"

"Where are they?" the enderman asks.

"They're just in my dad's workshop nearby," you say.

"Zombie workshop?" one of them asks.

"YES," you say. "It's a zombie workshop! Get over it!"

"Alright well where is it? We'll go take a look."

"Oh," you say. "Well, it's not that close. A very long walk. Too long."

"It's no problem," the enderman says. "We'll just teleport over and take a look and then come back and tell you what we think."

You stop dead.

Hadn't thought of that either…

"So where's this workshop?" the enderman presses.

You're sweating, green, zombie sweat.

"Uh, you know, I forget…" you say.

"What!?" the lead enderman says suspiciously. "You forgot where your dad's shop is!?"

"No…" you say. "Yes. I don't know."

"Are there even any mirrors? Or did you *lie to us?!*" The last part comes out as a menacing rasp.

"Uh, no, you know, there were no mirrors, but it wasn't a lie—"

The endermen don't want to hear the rest of your story. They're all staring at you and shaking angrily. Strange, evil sounds are escaping from their mouths, growing louder and louder.

You turn to run.

But it's too late.

No one survives the wrath of thirteen angry endermen.

THE END

To go back to the last choice and try again, *turn to page 104.*

To go back to the moment you returned to the surface and choose a new direction, *turn to page 57.*

Or, flip to the beginning and choose a new story!

You slip through the door and find yourself in a small, square room. The ceiling is made of wood, and there's a torch abandoned in the middle of the floor. One block of the floor is missing mysteriously.

You wander into the centre of the room, trying to decide what to do next. You turn around, looking at the three doors in the room.

Which one should you take?

Wait, which one did you come in from?

You rack your brain, trying to remember, but zombie brains, you are learning, are a little bit like goldfish brains. They both have *very* bad memories.

Okay, okay, you think, *I'm not a zombie, I'm a real kid, I can figure this out.*

Looking at the missing block on the floor, you think you figure out which of the three doors you entered by. You breath a big breath. That really freaked you out and you're still not *totally* sure that you're right.

If you want to retrace your steps to the room with five doors, *turn to page 72.*

If you want to take the door on the left, *turn to page 69.*

If you want to take the door on the right, *turn to page 89.*

"I'm so happy," you say to the old woman. But you turn to the endermen and mouth "Please, play along!" You put your hands together as if you were praying. The endermen's eyes just keep getting bigger.

One of the taller ones in the back, who seems to be a bit slower than the rest opens his mouth and says, "You're not our friend. We don't know—"

You are quickly and vigorously drawing your finger across your throat. That's the international symbol for "Please stop talking right now!"

The enderman stops talking with his mouth dangling open.

"What was that?" the woman asks. "You don't know Rotney? He said—"

"Well, what Roger over here was saying was that I'm not a friend, because I'm really more like your best friend, *right?*" You say the last word right to the tall enderman in the back.

"Noooo," says the enderman. "And my name's not Roger…"

"Ha ha ha," you laugh awkwardly.

"No, that's Eznetterrek," the old villager says. "I recognize his voice."

"Oh, I know!" you say, trying to cover your tracks. "I was just, uh— Roger is what we used to call him. A nickname. Like a short form of his name."

"How do you get Roger from Eznetterrek?" the old lady asks. "They don't sound anything alike."

"Well…" you say, drawing the word out really long, trying to think of something. But, you've got nothing.

"What's going on here?" The old lady squints.

"Nothing, nothing, nothing," you protest.

"Is this guy even your friend?" she asks the endermen.

"Honestly," one of the endermen in the front says, "we've never even seen this guy before."

The endermen are all looking at you. The old lady turns and joins them.

"Who. Are. You. Anyways?" she asks through tight lips.

A couple of the endermen's eyes begin to flash red. *Not a good sign.*

"You know? I've got to go," you say.

And then you turn and run. You don't look back, just in case the endermen are following you. And you don't stop running.

Not until you're far away and your legs are begging you to stop. You look around. You don't recognize anything. You're totally lost.

You have no idea how to get back to the village and the golem and the portal. You have no idea how to get *home*.

You turn and wander off into the wild world.

THE END

To go back to the last choice and try again, *turn to page 8*.

To go back to the moment you returned to the surface and choose a new direction, *turn to page 57*.

Or, flip to the beginning and choose a new story!

This door takes you to a small room that looks slightly familiar, or does it just look a little like every other room that you've found yourself in?

This room has two other doors as well.

You try to focus. You need to remember how you got here. Which door did you take to get in here? Which door did you take before that?

It was a left, right? A right? No, a left? I was just saying 'right?'. So, right? No, LEFT!

You're talking to yourself now. That can't be good.

And before that… it was a right? No, straight maybe…

You take a deep breath. What should you do now?

If you take the door on the right, *turn to page 22.*

If you take the door on the left, *turn to page 35.*

"Why are you guys hanging out here anyways? Seems like a pretty watery place for people who hate water," you say kindly.

"Well, if you hadn't noticed, it's much better than out *there*." One of the endermen nods towards the curtains of rain that are following outside the cover of the massive stone arch.

"Oh right, falling water…" you say thoughtfully.

"Basically our worst nightmare," the enderman says.

"But why right here?" you say looking around the hill.

"It's the furthest spot from any lake, stream or raindrop in the whole area," the enderman says morosely. "But it's still pretty bad." He makes a gross face while staring at the nearest lake. "We still have to look at it."

You look around. He's right. This place really is as far from a piece of water as you can possibly get. "You really can't do any better than this?" you ask.

"Not for many days in any direction. That's why we're all here." He waves his gangly arms at the huddle of endermen.

You realize they look a bit like a very small and very dense forest of skinny, black trees.

"We wish we had a better place." The enderman filled your silence. "Someplace dry and covered from the rain."

"Yeah," another enderman cut in. "Like those things the villagers have with the roofs and the walls and those wooden thing that swing open to get in…" The enderman searches for the word.

"Buildings?" you ask.

"Yes! Biddelings, exactly!" the second enderman says.

"We tried to build one," the first enderman says. He holds out the block in his hands. You hadn't noticed it before, but all the endermen are holding blocks. Most of these blocks are grey and speckled with shining green…

"But we just made that." The enderman nods at a weird looking pile of stone blocks on the other side of the hill. There are several green dots peaking out of those blocks too. Your player brain starts hyperventilating. "It's harder than it looks," the enderman remarks.

"You built it with emerald ore? That's your first problem…" you say.

The enderman stares down at the block in his hands. "Oh, guess so. I forget that all you upworlders like some rocks because of the way they look. They're all rocks…"

You suppose that's true.

"We can't place the blocks above our heads! It just won't work. We can't make ceilings. So here we are," the enderman says sadly.

"Well…" you say. "Why don't you just go stay with the villagers during a storm then?"

You almost have a heart attack as the endermen start making this terrible hacking sound all at once.

"Ahh! Ahh! Ahh!" you shout, looking all around you. "What's happening."

"Oh that's funny!" one of the enderman gasps between hacks. "But villagers are petrified of us! No way they'd let that happen. And anyways, they're always looking at us, making us feel self-conscious!"

That… was laughter? Enderman are weird…

You ponder for a second, trying to think of how to solve the problem and also how to get your ender pearls. Hopefully both at the same time.

If you offer to talk to the villagers for them, in exchange for their pearls, *turn to page 93*.

If you offer to build a house for them in exchange for their pearls, *turn to page 101*.

This room is smaller than the last one. There are emeralds shining from one of the walls and in the other corner of the room, a big crater suggests that a creeper has been here recently and seems to have gotten a *little* too excited.

At first you don't think that there's anything else too special in this room. But as you follow around the wall, dragging your right hand along the stone, you notice something very special about this room…

You come to the first door and knock lightly on the wood.

Then you find the second door. The sound of zombies reaches your ears. You're half-intrigued, half-scared.

And then your fingertips land on another wooden surface: a *third* door. And then you find two more after that…

The fourth door is actually a grand double door.

The fifth door is made of iron. A button beside the door invites you to push it.

You take a step back and decide what to do.

If you take the first door, *turn to page 47.*

If you take the second door, *turn to page 92.*

If you take the third door, *turn to page 50.*

If you take the fourth door, *turn to page 28.*

If you take the fifth door, *turn to page 113.*

A button is staring at you from the wall beside the cell.

Who would it hurt just to let this poor little spider out?

"Hey buddy," you say. "Don't worry about it. I'm going to get you out of there."

You hope that spiders can understand zombie language.

The spider just hurls itself at the bars again. *So I guess that's a 'no',* you think.

You click the button and the bars swing open all of a sudden. And just as they do, the spider leaps forward. Without the bars stopping it, it hits you in the chest and knocks you onto your back. You get a face full of hairy spider legs.

"Hey, hey!" you sputter. "Take it easy."

The spider legs are all over you. Once you shove it off, you try to struggle to your feet. But the spider isn't done. It leaps again. Hitting you right in the back, you stumble forward a couple steps.

"Hey! Little buddy, I know you're excited, but you've got to calm down." you say.

The spider just stares with its beady red eyes and leaps again. You fall down. As you look up, you notice that you're now on the other side of the prison door, inside the cell.

That's probably an accident though, right?, you think.

The spider leaps again. It seems like he's just jumping as wildly as he had before. But there's something different this time. He doesn't jump for you, but at the wall beside the cell instead.

And one of its legs hits the button.

CLANG! The bars swing shut.

"Hey! Hey!" you say, bouncing to your feet and rattling the door. "Jump again, hit the button!"

But the spider has stopped jumping. It's just staring at you.

"Now it'sssss your turn," it hisses.

"What? What?!" you shout.

But the spider is gone, crawling down the hallway.

"WHAT?!" you scream. It echoes down the empty corridor.

THE END

To go back to the last choice and try again, *turn to page 28.*

To go back to the beginning of the maze and try again, *turn to page 8.*

Or, flip to the beginning and choose a new story!

"Endermen are tall, right?" you ask yourself. "So they probably like being in tall places."

With the rain still pelting down, you walk to the base of the arch and start climbing up. Once you're on the arch, it's impossible to even tell that it's an arch anymore. It just looks like a mountain. The top of it is so massive that it seems to spread out in every direction.

You take a zigzag path up the arch, keeping your eyes peeled for any endermen. The forest is quite thick here though and you can't see very far in any one direction. You hear some hissing from nearby and follow the sounds, but it's just a couple spiders climbing some trees and quite upset about the rain. You're worried at first that you'll have to fight them off. But they just look at you and then keep climbing.

You *are* a zombie after all.

For once grateful that you're a zombie, you keep climbing the arch until you seem to have reached the top. You weave through the forest until you're at the edge of the arch and you stare down at the world around you.

It's beautiful!

You can see everything!

Little villages and rivers and lakes dot the land beneath you. Even the mountains that surround the arch look small in comparison. You see a couple players building a tower on a nearby hill. You also spot the village that you just left. You can just make out the hole in the ground that you came out of.

No endermen though. It's weird. You can see some creepers and spiders and jellies out on the plains beneath. But not a single enderman. *What's going on?*

You keep walking and find yourself in a bit of a clearing. Near the edge of the arch something catches your eye: it's tall and black!

At last!

You run towards it. "Enderman! Enderman!" you shout.

But the enderman doesn't say anything. As you get closer, you realize why: the enderman is just a tree. It's missing all of it's leaves and has dark bark.

Dangit...

Maybe you just went the wrong way. Maybe you should check under the arch instead. You know there aren't any endermen out on the plains, but you can't see under the arch itself. You really don't want to have to walk all the way down. Peering over the edge of the arch you think you might be able to take a shortcut by walking right along the edge and dropping into the trees below.

If you take the shortcut, *turn to page 108.*

If you go back and walk under the arch, *turn to page 109.*

Very quietly, so as not to scare her, you walk up behind her.

She doesn't turn and notice you. She just struggles to pick a pumpkin from it's stalk.

Don't scare her.

It's a hard thing to do when your body is literally designed to scare people. You sidestep very slowly so that you're in her field of vision and wave softly.

She yanks up on the pumpkin, but it doesn't budge. For a second, she's looking right at you. But she doesn't even seem to notice. She just goes back to yanking.

You clear your throat. "Hello?" you say as quietly as you can manage.

Now she looks up. "Who's that?" she asks sharply. "You'll have to forgive an old lady. My eyes don't work, you see... is that Bertrand or Asparagi?"

She can't see you, that's why she didn't run!

"No..." you say hesitantly.

"Giddyup, is that you dear?"

"Uh no, we've actually never met," you say.

"A newcomer!" she says excitedly. "Well welcome!" and she steps forward and wraps you in a hug.

It's very surprising. You don't move a muscle.

She sniffs. "You should take a shower, and you need to work on your hugs."

You sigh a relieved sigh. "You're right ma'am." Then you realize something: she can understand you! You're speaking zombie and she understands, amazing!

"So why are you here, dear? Need a place to stay?" she brushes her dirty hands off on her dress.

"Kind of," you say. "I'm actually looking for a house for some friends of mine."

"Sure, we have a spare home on the outskirts. They can have it, no problem, as long as they work in the gardens with the rest of us!" she says happily.

"Uh okay, well, there's a couple things. They only want the house when it's raining..."

The old woman is clearly surprised. "Ooookay, strange..." she says.

"That's not the weirdest part," you say. "They're also... endermen..."

The old lady's eyes grew almost as big as an enderman's. "What?! Why would we ever do a thing like that?!"

Moment of truth, you think. *Come on, think! Why* would *they do a thing like that?*

If you tell her the endermen will pay, *turn to page 125.*

If you tell her the endermen will attack if they don't, *turn to page 100.*

It's best to be careful. And anyways, you're curious.

You approach the paper in the corner. As you get closer, you realize that it isn't just *any* paper, it's a map!

You get right up next to it and look at it closely. It's showing a big, complicated building with many rooms and winding corridors. It hurts your eyes to even look at it.

Once you get over the dizzying labyrinth in front of you, you notice one room is marked with '*You are here*'. You put your finger on it. In another corner of the map there's a room marked with a star.

I wonder what that means, you think.

You trace your finger along the path between where you are and the room with the star. If you leave through the door in the other corner, you'll go to a room with five doors exiting it. You have to take the second door from the right and go down the hallway into another small room. And then you need to take the door on the left which will take you to another room where you have to go right. And then you'll go left again and enter a corridor. Take the third door on the right and go down some stairs and you'll end up at the room with a star.

Can you remember all that?

You look again and then head for the door.

To go through the door, *turn to page 72.*

"Off we go," you say to yourself as you reach the curtain of rain on the far side of the arch.

With a deep breath you step out into the rain and keep exploring.

You spot some more players building a large tower on top of a nearby hill. One speaks to the other. You can't hear what they're saying over the sound of the rain. But their words do hover over their heads in white text. You squint your eyes to read it:

"WATCH OUT FOR MOBS IN THE RAIN. THOSE PESKY SKELLIES AND ZOMBIES COULD BE ANYWHERE!"

You turn around and head the other direction.

Hours later, and you're still searching. You haven't seen a single enderman. Night falls and the rain stops and you keep walking and walking and walking.

Some zombies call to you to join them in their scaring, but you skitter off in the other direction, not wanting to talk to anyone.

You find a cave to hide in as day breaks.

It's two days later when you finally see an enderman standing on a nearby hill. *Finally*. You look around to see how far from the arch and the village you are, but something's off.

You can't see the arch anywhere. You're *that* far away.

You're *totally* lost.

You let the enderman wander away. There's no point. Not when you're this lost.

You head off into the night again, desperate to find home.

THE END

To go back to the last choice and try again, *turn to page 62*.

To go back to the moment you returned to the surface and choose a new direction, *turn to page 57*.

Or, flip to the beginning and choose a new story!

Probably not the best to ask for help from the one villager who's not even smart enough to run away...

"Come back here!" you shout. "I don't mean you any harm! I just want to ask you a question!"

The growls and moans come pouring out of your mouth and the villagers just start running faster.

You follow after them, running after the biggest herd of panicked villagers. For a little while, they run and you follow. Your legs are getting tired. *Maybe this wasn't the best move...*

But just as you think that, a couple of the villagers who are farthest away stop running.

Finally.

They huddle together with a couple of the other villagers and then turn to face you. *They've come to their senses! Great!*

You walk right up to them. "Hey guys! I'm glad that you've finally decided to talk to me—"

But as you say it, you notice something shiny in one of their hands... it's a hoe! And another one is holding a shovel! And all at once they're running right at you!

"Hey, wait, what—" you say, but they're all around you in a second.

"Get out of here icky zombie!" one of them shouts.

"We will avenge our village," another screams as she raises her hoe over her head. And then she has the nerve to smack it down right on your head.

"OW! Hey!" you yell.

But before you can say anything else, you take a shovel to the stomach and then a pickaxe in the back.

It doesn't take too many more hits before your soft, zombie body poofs out of existence, never to be seen again.

THE END

To go back to the last choice and try again, *turn to page 38. Or flip to the beginning and choose a new story!*

Well, at least she isn't running.

As the rest of the villagers scatter over the surrounding fields, you take a couple careful steps up to the old lady, who is still staring at the wall. You go slow, trying not to spook her.

You want to put your hands out to show that you don't mean any harm, but your hands are already out...

Slowly, carefully you approach the old lady.

She doesn't really seem to notice you.

You take a couple more steps and now you're *right* beside her. She *still* doesn't seem to notice you.

What's wrong with this lady?

You get so close that you can smell her. Besides smelling like delicious person (a weird side-effect of the whole being-a-zombie thing), she smells like daisies and campfires. It's nice.

She turns towards you, at last. But she doesn't scream or run. Instead of the normal green eyes of a villager, she has grey eyes. They don't focus on you but stare off into space.

Maybe she can't see?

If you want to talk to her, *turn to page 52.*

If you try to communicate silently, *turn to page 91.*

"Well, here's the thing," you say. "Those people that you met… you know they weren't just really tall people with really bad colds. They were actually… well, they were endermen."

Her eyebrows arch wildly.

"Don't freak out," you beg her.

"Those weren't… people?" she asks. "Those were endermen? Those were monsters?"

"Well… Yeah," you say. "Sorry."

"But they were so nice!" she says.

"I mean sometimes monsters are nice," you say with a little smile on your lips. *Just look at me.*

She thinks again for a second. "How do you know?" she shoots at you.

"What?" you ask.

"How do you know, for sure, that they're endermen. Why can't they just be a couple tall people that talked weird and had strange habits?" She puts her hands on her hips.

"Well, just… no one really talks that weird. When you meet a "person" like that… it's actually a mob. I promise you. That's why they talk weird. People like that just don't exist…" You try to tell her softly.

Suddenly, even though she can't see you, the woman looks up and meets your eyes. She's staring right into you and seeing nothing. "What about you?"

You swear, your heart stops beating. Oh wait, maybe it wasn't beating in the first place… After all, you're dead… and in a video game. Your eyes are locked on her face.

"You," she says, getting louder and louder with each word. "You're a stranger that I met out of nowhere. And you talk strange, just like those others that I met earlier…"

"No, no," you protest. "I just talk weird," you say. You need her help!

"People that talk that weird just don't exist… do they?" she asks wickedly. "You're a monster, just like those things that I met in the woods," she continues, putting it all together. "What are you trying to do to me? Why are you here?" Her confidence turns to fear. She starts stumbling backwards, trying to escape.

"No, no, I'm not going to hurt you. I'm not going to eat your brains!" you protest.

"You're a zombie!" She turns and starts running and screaming. She smacks right into a tree. You kind of laugh, and then feel bad about it.

Her screams attract the attention of the villagers that ran off earlier. They're brave enough to come back to her aid. They grab her and help her to her feet. They talk for a second and then all turn to face you.

Uh oh.

And then in a second, they're all running right at you.

Now it's your turn to run away. You run as fast as your rotting legs will take you, until you can't take another step.

You look back, you've lost the villagers. But you have no idea where you are. You're lost in the world of minecraft. Just another zombie with no way to get home and no one to help you…

THE END

To go back to the last choice and try again, *turn to page 48*.

To go back to the moment you returned to the surface and choose a new direction, *turn to page 57*.

Or, flip to the beginning and choose a new story!

You stop walking.

"Okay," you say. "You didn't really answer the question. What's the prophecy? The 'Chosen One', they were brought back to do what? You didn't say."

The golem slows and then stops and then spins around towards you.

"WHAT? DID YOU SAY?" the golem's voice almost knocked you over. It boomed and bounced off the hills, echoing all around you.

"Tell me the prophecy," you say. You try to match his booming voice. But you just sound like a mouse to his lion's roar.

The golem looks down over its nose. "No. I have told you everything you need to know. All that you need to do now is follow me. I'll show you everything you need to do. I'll show you how to get home."

"But you think I'm the Chosen One," you say. "You have to tell me."

"I have to tell you nothing. I've told you exactly what you need to know. No more. No less. When you need to know more, I'll make sure you know it." The golem turns and starts walking. "Now, follow."

It feels almost impossible to not obey that booming voice. Your zombie feet lurch after the giant stone golem as you approach the village.

The second that the villagers of this town see the golem, they start running. One runs right past you, its long, silly nose flopping against its face with every step.

You try to hold in a giggle but it escapes. It comes out like an elephant choking on a peanut: "Grawwwwwakakaka." It's easy to forget that you're a zombie.

The golem isn't interested in the villagers though, instead it goes to the well in the centre of town and with a big swing of one of its stone fists it clears a chunk of dirt from the opening of the well.

The golem looks at you. "Dig," it says.

You nod at your weird little arms sticking right out in front of your face. "Can't," you say.

"Useless zombies," the golem says.

"Hey, I didn't ask for this," you remind him.

With another couple swings of his arms, he starts descending down into the hole he is digging. You hop from block to block, following the golem down.

A moment later, he swings his fist and you see a tiny hole in the solid stone beneath you. There's something down there! A chamber of some sort.

With a finger, the golem daintily clears away more rock until there's an entrance big enough to walk through.

"Come," he booms and enters the passageway.

You follow after him and when your eyes adjust to the gloom on the other side (luckily zombie eyes are great at seeing in the dark) you see a medieval looking chamber with two doors leading out of it. This isn't just some cavern. You recognize this place, you've seen something like it on servers before. This is a *stronghold*...

"Go," the golem says. "I'm too large to fit through the doors. You must go. Find a room with lava, shout for me, and I'll follow you."

If you go through the door on the right, *turn to page 8*.

If you go through the door on the left, *turn to page 23*.

With your hands out and open to show that you're not threatening, you walk towards the scared huddle of villagers.

They see you and point. "Zombie! He's reaching out to try to eat our brains!"

The villagers begin to run, their long noses flopping with every step.

"No!" you shout. "No!"

This just scares them more.

You're happy to note that not all the villagers run. A couple have stayed in place. They are facing each other in a tight little huddle.

"Hey guys!" you say happily. "Thanks for sticking around."

They turn to you as you talk. Each one of them is holding something: a hoe, a shovel, a pickaxe. One even has a sword. A wooden sword, but still!

"Uh oh, guys," you say. "No need for that."

But they ignore you. One screams and runs towards you.

"No, no, no, no," you shout.

He thwacks you on the head with his hoe. The world starts to spin. You don't notice, in the haze, the other villagers surrounding you and whacking at you with their various tools.

"Ow, ow, ow, ow!" you shout.

The world fades out.

THE END

To go back to the last choice and try again, *turn to page 93*.

To go back to the moment you returned to the surface and choose a new direction, *turn to page 57*.

Or, flip to the beginning and choose a new story!

Honesty is the best policy, that's what your mom always says.

"I need something they have," you say. "I need ender pearls… twelve of them…"

For a second, the woman processes what you said. You know the exact moment that she understands, because her eyes grow wide.

"Twelve of them?!" she exclaims. "Or did I misunderstand?'"

"No, you heard me right," you groan.

"Wow, well that won't be easy," the old lady says. "I've never met an enderman—"

Or at least you don't think you have… you think. *Just like you've never met a zombie?*

"—But," she continues. "I hear they're pretty protective of those pearl things. People say they're quite pretty. People say that you can only get one if you *kill* the enderman." She whispers this last part as if it were a secret.

"Yeah," you say, finally remembering not to just nod. "But I need them for something important. I need them to get home, so I've got to try!"

She looks at you and pauses for a second. She doesn't ask you for more details, or question you at all. She just nods solemnly and says, "I understand. The most important thing of all. Well, like I said, I've never met an enderman, so I can't really help you find any…"

Your shoulders slump. *Dangit.*

"But," the lady continues, "I do know a different way you might be able to get some ender pearls! Some of the travelling merchants from the other villages sell them sometimes. If you want, I can take you to my friend, he's a merchant and he may be able to sell you some… if you can pay."

You purse your green lips.

If you go with her to the merchant, *turn to page 39*.

If you try to find out if she *has* actually met an enderman, *turn to page 48*.

This door takes you to a small room that looks slightly familiar, or does it just look a little like every other room that you've found yourself in?

This room has two other doors as well.

You try to focus. You need to remember how you got here. Which door did you take to get in here? Which door did you take before that?

It was a left, right? A right? No, a left? I was just saying 'right?'. So, right? No, LEFT!

You're talking to yourself now. That can't be good.

And before that… it was a right? No, straight maybe…

You take a deep breath. What should you do now?

If you take the door on the right, *turn to page 35*.

If you take the door on the left, *turn to page 22*.

With your eyes fixed to the chest, you step up the golden stairs and climb to the top of the altar in the centre of the room. The gold steps feel slippery under your feet and you have to go carefully to keep your footing.

The chest sits in front of you now, begging you to open it. Not like literally, but you get what I mean.

You place your finger on the little red dot above the lock and try to rub it off.

That's weird. It doesn't come off. It's not paint or blood. *So what is it?*

You try to brush it off and put your hands on either side of the chest's lid and lift. There's a weird click as you open the chest.

An old chest, you think. *Must be.* But then you notice a little explosion of red dust floating in the air.

That can't be good…

You glance into the chest and see a couple gleaming gold items: a sword, some armour, and weirdly… a fish… You don't have time to think about it much though, before you see something in your peripheral vision.

Holes have opened in the walls on either side of you and something fires quickly out of them: arrows!

One thought passes through your mind before the arrows hit you.

Dang, a trapped chest.

And the next second, you're a zombie pin cushion.

THE END

To go back to the last choice and try again, *turn to page 113.* Or flip to the beginning and choose a new story!

You can't let on that you're a zombie. If you open your mouth, the only thing that will come out is angry, undead growls.

You wave at her nicely. She doesn't seem to notice.

You try doing what you had to do last time you needed to talk with a player: hopping in morse code. Morse code is an old way that people used to communicate with electronic signals. All the words are made of short taps and long taps. If you jump in the proper pattern then maybe she'll understand you.

You jump out the phrase, "Do you understand me?" and wait for her to respond. She just looks vaguely past you.

"Hello?" she says. "Is there someone there?"

You wave again.

"Hello?" she says, confused.

This isn't working.

Maybe you'll have better luck with someone else.

If you want to follow those fleeing villagers, *turn to page 81.*

If you want to go explore near the giant stone arch, *turn to page 46.*

There's a long hallway here.

Trying to tiptoe as best you can with your zombie feet, you sneak down the corridor. You're not very successful. Every time you try to tiptoe, you just smack your heavy shoes into the stone floor.

CLOMP, CLOMP, CLOMP, go your feet as you creep down the hallway. Whatever's at the end of this hallway has *definitely* heard you coming.

You get to the end and put your hand on the wooden door there. It's cracked open slightly. Slowly you open it wider so that you can see inside, then you peek in. You open it one inch, then two, but you can't see anything through the crack. Finally you push it open all at once and you freeze in horror.

Eight zombies fill the room, wandering around aimlessly. But when they see you, they all turn and moan at once.

GRAAAAAUUUURRRGGHHHHHHHnngg, they say.

This is where the noise was coming from, you realize.

A couple of them stumble towards you. Panic starts to flutter in your chest. You have to do something, *now!*

If you turn and run, *turn to page 54.*

If you talk to the zombies, *turn to page 3.*

"Hey, tell you what," you say. "I'll go talk to the villagers for you... if you pay me."

"You? Talk to the villagers? You're not any better," the enderman says while looking you up and down.

"I think I can do it, trust me," you say.

The endermen stare. You imagine they'd be raising their eyebrows... if they had eyebrows.

"Well, anyways, even if you can," the enderman says, sounding defeated. "We don't have anything to pay you with. No player flesh here..."

"No, no, that's not what I want," you say. "I want ender pearls. Twelve of them. You have those."

The endermen are shocked. They are all looking at each other.

The enderman opens his mouth to speak and then closes it and turns back to the rest of his huddle. They lean in and talk quietly.

After a second they turn back. "Fine," he says. "If for some reason you can get us a spot in the village during future storms, we'll give you our pearls."

A couple of the endermen let out some raspy snickers. They clearly don't believe you can do it.

You swallow hard. "Deal," you say.

You turn back towards the village and start walking. You have no idea how, but *some*how, you'll get this done.

You haven't come up with any good ideas before the village appears in the distance. *Let's wing it,* you think to yourself and march right into the village.

The villagers are, again, making their way back into the village. They're herding their children into houses and cleaning up the roads. Some of them are trying to fill in the hole that's ruined their village square.

And then they see you, and turn and run for the far end of the village.

These guys are just having a terrible day, you think.

You watch them all gather in a scared little huddle behind the biggest house. Well, almost all of them. One old lady is wandering around her vegetable garden, seemingly unaware that anything is happening at all.

You know you need to talk to the leaders of the town if you're going to get anything done, and they probably *are* in that huddle…

If you approach the scared villagers, *turn to page 87*.

If you approach the old woman, *turn to page 77*.

You think about it.

"No!" you say. "I don't have to apologize for being a zombie! I'll eat people if I want to!"

The old lady looks shocked.

"Yeah, that's right!" you say. "Maybe I'll eat you!"

Her face turns to horror and she slams the door in your face.

Fine, I didn't need her anyways, you think. *It's not like I could pay for anything anyways. I'm a zombie! I'M A ZOMBIE!*

You stomp off into the night.

The nerve of her, to make me promise not to eat someone! I'll do what I want to! If you're going to help me, don't try to control me!

After a short walk you see a player in the distance. They don't seem to have much armour on and there is no shelter that you can see nearby.

Ohhhh, Madame Mole wouldn't want me to eat you, you think.

Half-joking, you start creeping up behind the player. The poor guy looks like a bit of a noob. He's just chopping down some trees. He doesn't even notice you. Not when you're right behind him.

I could bite you right now, and you wouldn't be able to do a thing about it!

He suddenly looks around, sees you, and comes running at you with his wooden axe. Instinctually you grab at him and bite! Your teeth sink into his block-shaped flesh.

He punches you in the stomach which makes you mad. You bite again. And again and again. And soon he collapses onto the ground.

It feels good! You're empowered by eating someone! You want to do it again!

You wander off into the night, looking for more players to eat...

THE END

To go back to the last choice and try again, *turn to page 51.*

To go back to the moment you returned to the surface and choose a new direction, *turn to page 57.*

Or, flip to the beginning and choose a new story!

The way that the endermen scuttle away from you gives you an idea. If they really hate getting splashed that much, then they might be willing to do something to make you stop.

You skip around the circle of endermen, making sure to land heavy in the wet grass. Droplets of water land all around the endermen making them shriek and shimmy away from you.

"Stop that!" one of the endermen rasps. "You're getting us wet!"

"Oh you don't like that, right!" you say, playing dumb. "I'm just so happy to see you guys! I can't help myself."

"Wh-why? Why are you so excited to see us?" the enderman asks.

"Oh, because I've been looking for something. Ender pearls! I thought you guys could help me." You skip a little further around the circle.

The endermen scowl even harder now, waddling away from you more quickly.

"Ender pearls?" the same enderman asks suspiciously. "So you want our pearls?"

"Oh, you guys have some?" you ask.

"Of course, everyone knows that every enderman has an ender pearl," the enderman snarls.

"I'm just a zombie," you moan. "I don't know that much."

"Okay…"

"Anyways," you say. "I wouldn't want to take *your* pearls. I just want some of my own."

"Well, I don't know anyway of getting one without getting one from an enderman. When we arrive on this plain, we bring one with us…" the enderman says.

This isn't working, you decide to skip a little more.

"Stop it!" one of the endermen snaps.

You come to a halt suddenly, a little scared. You swallow and work up your courage.

"Sorry, I'd leave in a second if I just had the twelve pearls I need…" you say. "But until then, I just gotta keep skipping!"

"Are you, are you threatening us?!" the enderman rasps loudly.

Uh oh, these guys are smarter than you thought. You chuckle nervously. "Oh no, just stating the facts."

The endermen don't do anything but stare at you.

Fine. You start skipping again to show them that you're serious.

"STOP!" the endermen shout together.

You just swallow and keep going. You *need* these pearls.

"Alright!" the lead enderman says. "That's it! Let's do it guys."

All at once the huddle of endermen stop scuttling away from you and instead right towards you and charge with their arms lifted.

Uh oh, is the last thought you ever have.

THE END

To go back to the last choice and try again, *turn to page 44.*

To go back to the moment you returned to the surface and choose a new direction, *turn to page 57.*

Or, flip to the beginning and choose a new story!

Your brain works quickly. *She can't suspect anything…*

"Well, of course getting home is important," you say. "I mean, that's what I'm all about. It's terrible to be alone…" You hold on the pause for a second, hanging your head low.

The old woman feels that sadness in your voice. She looks like she could cry.

"But those friends," you say, pretending to regain the strength to talk. "They're almost like family to me. They're old, long lost friends. If I could find them again, well. Maybe I wouldn't need to get back home anymore. Maybe I could make a new home here…"

You peek at the woman's face. It looks like your sob story has worked.

"Okay," she says. "You're right. I don't know why I didn't think of that. Of course, of course, I'll take you to them! Who would I be if I didn't!"

You feel a little bad for tricking an old, blind lady, but she might be too scared to take you if she knew the truth. She might start expecting *you*… No, this is what you'd have to do to get home.

The old woman hooks her arm around yours and asks what you see around you. You tell her the landmarks, and based on that, she tells you which way to go.

It's a bit of a zigzag path that you take through the wilderness outside the town. You're moving through the hills. The woman is guiding you to walk towards a mountain peak far away that looks like a bird's beak. When you pass a forest, she gets you to turn left and you walk out onto a massive, empty plateau.

"We're close," she says. "Do you see some ruins near here?"

You do. There is a broken down castle nearby that someone must have built a *long* time ago.

You walk towards it and then together you climb up the decaying stairs to the roof.

"They should be here," she says.

You cross your fingers as you pop up onto the roof. *Come on, come on, come on.*

You look around.

There's nothing here, but broken stone and a couple trees that are growing in the dirt that has settled up here… No endermen.

"Nothing," you say. "They must have left. I guess it makes sense… That *was* a while ago."

"Don't lose hope yet," the old woman says.

But you have. You sit down on a nearby stone and pout.

"Friends…" the old lady calls. "Friends!"

And then suddenly you hear a strange electronic noise.

You look up to see a tall, black shape standing near the old lady.

You look back down right away. *Endermen.*

A couple other strange cosmic noises announce the arrival of a few more. And then a few more.

A whole crowd is gathered around the woman now.

"Come friend, come!" she says excitedly. "They're here!"

They are.

Now, how are you going to get those pearls?

If you surprise attack the endermen, *turn to page 102.*

If you go over to meet them, *turn to page 41.*

"Well," you say, "the question is not why *would* you, but why *wouldn't* you. If you don't let them have the house, well, they'll take it from you anyways!"

"What are you saying?" the old woman asks with narrowed eyes.

"Well, I'm here to help you," you say. "I heard the endermen saying that they were going to come attack and take your houses, so I thought that I'd come and help you. If you offer them a house they won't have to attack and take one themselves. I'm just trying to protect you."

She doesn't look very grateful for your selfless move. "*This* is what you call helping?" she asks. "Threatening us?"

"No, I'm trying to—" You are interrupted by a roar from behind you. It's a hoard of angry villagers.

"GET AWAY FROM GRANDMA MOLE," the leader of the hoard yells, "YOU MONSTER!"

The villagers are waving weapons and tools viciously.

"No, no, I'm not attacking her," you say in a panic. You turn to the old lady. "Tell them that I'm not hurting you! Tell them what I said!"

She raises an eyebrow. "Why would I help *you?*"

"No, but—"

And that is the moment that you're completely surrounded by angry villagers. You don't last long in the violent onslaught of hoes hitting you in the head.

THE END

To go back to the last choice and try again, *turn to page 77.*

To go back to the moment you returned to the surface and choose a new direction, *turn to page 57.*

Or, flip to the beginning and choose a new story!

"Hey guys," you say. "I've got an idea."

They all stare with their headlight eyes.

"If I can build you a house, will you do me a favour?" you ask.

"You could build a house?" they ask.

"Sure," you say, "I've built a hundred before."

They are looking very suspicious now, but the one in front says, "Suuuuuuure? What's the favour?"

"I need twelve ender pearls," you say. "It's for something very important."

The enderman all turn to each other and start rasping and growling under their breath. After a second, they turn back towards you. Those unsettling big eyes are all beaming at you. You kind of liked it better when they *weren't* looking.

"Sure," the enderman says. "If you can build us a house, then we'll give you the pearls, but only then!"

"It's a deal," you say with a smile. And you get to work.

If you want to make a wood pickaxe first, *turn to page 112.*

If you want to start digging first, *turn to page 18.*

There's only one way to get a pearl from an enderman, as far as *you* know. And nothing's going to stop you from getting back home. Here goes!

You're up in a second and charging towards the endermen. The thing with attacking endermen is that they are sneaky. They can teleport. So you need the element of surprise. That's the only way to be sure you'll hit them.

The woman is talking to the endermen. They seem fascinated by her. Each of them has put down the block they were carrying and is watching the old woman carefully. This works for you, because none of them even notice that you're here until you're right on top of them. You choose the enderman closest to you and sink your teeth into its black flesh.

Biting in is a… strange sensation. It's a little bit like biting into a giant fish. Yeah, that's right. An enderman tastes a little like really stinky fish, a little like brand new tires and feels a little bit like eating a mouthful of pins and needles. *Weird.*

The enderman makes a raspy scream noise. You realize, with a smile, that your impression of them earlier was pretty good.

You pull back and bite again.

This time it tastes very different.

It tastes like… nothing at all.

You open your eyes.

You're not biting an enderman. You're biting open space. There's no enderman where there was one a second ago.

An enderman has suddenly appeared at the other end of the roof.

Dangit, teleportation is just not fair.

But there's plenty of other endermen all around you. You leap at another one to bite it. But the element of surprise is gone. They're all watching you now. And as you move towards them, they all vanish at once. Suddenly, they're scattered around the roof.

"What's happening? What's happening?" the old lady asks frantically.

You don't have time to answer. You set your sights on the closest enderman and charge. As you take your fourth step, you feel a searing pain in your back. You turn around. There's an enderman behind you.

Or rather there was. As soon as you look at it, it's gone.

But there *is* an enderman behind you now. It's just teleported behind you and it strikes down at you with its long arms.

You're getting faint.

You spin back around to see six other enderman suddenly appear all around you.

The last thought that you remember having is: *Maybe this wasn't such a great idea.*

THE END

To go back a couple choices and try again, *turn to page 98.*

To go back to the moment you returned to the surface and choose a new direction, *turn to page 57.*

Or, flip to the beginning and choose a new story!

"Oh you know," you say, swallowing. "Hey! Has anybody told you guys that you look great? Like, you're all really handsome, pretty, beautiful."

They're all staring at you still with their bugged out eyes. It feels like standing in the centre of a circle of nine foot tall, black goldfish.

"You know that's why I came," you say. "That's why I was looking for you. Because they say that you're a very attractive bunch. And they weren't lying!"

Silence hangs in the air for a second and then one of the endermen waves their long black arms bashfully.

"No," they say. "You're just saying that!"

You smile. It's working. "No, I'm not, for real, you guys all look great. Love the black. The tall, elegant thing… It's really working for you!"

A couple of the endermen laugh timidly, or at least that's what you think it is. It sounds like an old man coughing on a mouthful of stale crackers.

"Thanks," one of them says quietly.

"I don't know," says another, taking a black, shiny orb mysteriously from somewhere on their body. They hold it out in front of them staring at it. "I just think that my legs are too long sometimes, you know?"

It's an ender pearl! What are they doing with it?

Another takes out their own pearl, holding it in front of them. "I think my eyes are too small," this one says.

That's when it clicks.

"Oh! You use those as a mirror!" you say. You didn't mean to say it out loud. But whatever…

"Yes, yes," says the enderman in front, pulling out their own pearl. "It's the only thing that works. You see normal mirrors… we're always too tall for them! We can never see our feet!"

"Or our heads!" another adds.

"True," says the one in front. "But the curved surface of this lets us see everything. Very useful."

All of the endermen have taken out their pearls now. You count quickly in your head. *1-2... 5-6-7... 12-13. There's enough! Just how to get them?*

The endermen seem to hardly know you're there anymore. They're all absorbed in their pearls, staring at themselves. They're hemming and hawing over their appearance. None of them believe that they look good!

You stare hungrily at the pearls, plotting.

If you tell them that looking in the pearls that much is bad for them, *turn to page 119.*

If you promise you can get them better mirrors in exchange for their pearls, *turn to page 64.*

"Alright," you say, "I'm going to be honest with you."

The endermen shuffle a little, watching you with their big eyes, like a bunch of really tall, really spooky owls.

"I'm here, because I need ender pearls. I need them, well… I need them to make a portal so that I can go home," you say quickly.

The endermen are looking at you with a mix of confusion and anger on their strange faces.

"It's too hard to explain," you say. "But the bottom line is that I need those ender pearls."

One of the endermen approaches you, raising themselves to their full height. "Well, you'll never get them! They're ours! You're just as bad as those pesky players that keep bothering us for our pearls!"

More than you know, you think.

"Right, well, I know you don't want to *give* them to me," you say. "But I think I might be able to convince you it's the best idea…"

The endermen are even more confused now. They are starting to shuffle more, moving back and forth quickly. "Impossible," one hisses.

"Well, here's the thing. If you *don't* give them to me, I'll tell the old lady what you really are!"

The endermen gasp and scream. "No!"

"She won't be coming back to hang out with you guys anytime soon…" you say with a satisfied smile. "So…" you add, sticking your hand out expectantly.

The endermen look at your hand and then at each other…

"There's only two choices," you say. "Choose one."

"Actually," rasps one of the endermen. "There's another choice…"

You look at the enderman. "What?"

The endermen answer your question by rushing at you all at once, their arms raised high in the air. All at once you're buried in a storm of flailing arms. Everything goes black.

THE END

To go back to the last choice and try again, *turn to page 110.*

To go back to the moment you returned to the surface and choose a new direction, *turn to page 57.*

Or, flip to the beginning and choose a new story!

You've taken hundreds of shortcuts like this before, when you were playing Minecraft, and anyways, you really want to get home as soon as possible.

You have to walk right along the edge of the big arch. That looks like the fastest way down. You hop a couple steps down onto the edge of the rock face. Looking down, you get dizzy. The ground is a *long* ways down.

Luckily, there are still a couple blocks between you and the very edge.

It's slow going with your clumsy zombie legs, but you keep hopping along the edge. The slope here gets steeper and steeper and you have no choice but to hop along the very last row of bricks before the drop.

This is fine, you encourage yourself. *I've done this a hundred times before.*

You hop down to the next block and think that it might have just been faster to walk around the long way.

You hop again, to the next block which is two blocks down. But you miss your footing and trip off the block. You throw out your arms to try to catch the edge of the arch. But you're too slow.

You plummet over the edge and towards the wetlands far below.

As you fall you just have one thought. *Sure, I've done this a hundred times before. But never with zombie feet…*

You look down and see a lake quickly approaching.

Oh, that's good, if I land in water it will cushion my fall.

But then a gust of wind hits you and blows you a little to the left.

Uh oh.

You don't land in the water.

You make a big zombie pancake on the shore of the lake.

So close.

THE END

To go back to the last choice and try again, *turn to page 75.*

To go back to the moment you returned to the surface and choose a new direction, *turn to page 57.*

Or, flip to the beginning and choose a new story!

You head out to the land underneath the arch. It's a long walk, but after a little time you're getting close. The edge of the arch is almost right above you.

In front of you there is a break in the rain. A place where it suddenly stops pouring down. You go a little further and you find yourself there. You put out your arms on either side of you. The rain is falling on your left hand but your right hand is dry. You made it.

Now, to find the endermen.

You start looking. The good news is that the land here is pretty flat and there are almost no trees. In fact there are almost no forests or hills at all because all the land beneath the arch seems to be swampy and covered in lakes and streams.

Your head is a lot dryer now that you're out of the rain, but your feet are a lot wetter.

Even though everything's pretty flat, a light fog lays over the whole land, making it hard to see very far.

You check out the south side of the land under the arch, weaving around all the water and occasionally wading through it. You find no endermen.

There's only one hill, in the centre of the land. And there is more wetlands beyond that.

If you want to go explore the hill, *turn to page 44.*

If you want to explore the wetlands on the other side, *turn to page 62.*

"Well, actually…" you say.

The old lady turns to you. Her old, wrinkled face is twisted in confusion.

"I have to come clean," you say. "These aren't actually my old friends. I'm not a villager and they're not—"

You get cut off halfway through the sentence by a loud explosion of rasping and screaming. The endermen are waving their arms and making gestures with their hands. One of them is repeatedly drawing their finger across their neck in the universal hand symbol for 'STOP! ABORT!'

Your mouth just hangs stupidly open.

"Ummm," you say.

"What? What are you saying?" the old woman asks. She turns to the endermen. "What's wrong?"

The endermen's eyes are as big as slimes. They're staring right at you (which is a little scary) and motioning with your hands for you to speak, for you to make something up.

"Umm," you say. "I'm not a villager, because you see, I belong here. And they're not my friends because…"

Everyone hangs in suspense.

"They're my family."

The endermen nod and shrug at you.

The old woman looks surprised.

"Yes," one of the endermen rasps. "He's right. This is our child, from long ago. We didn't recognize him because…"

Another one butts in. "He grew so much!"

"Yesss," the first one confirms.

"Wow," the old lady says, thinking it through. "Well, this is amazing! I'm so glad that I could be part of your reunion!" You think that you see tears welling in the corners of her eyes.

"I'll give you some privacy then," she says, backing up a couple steps. "I'm sure that you all want to talk, after so long…"

She excuses herself and goes to stand by the edge of the roof, feeling the wind on her face.

You check to make sure that she really is out of ear shot and then you turn back to the endermen. You are a little startled to find them all staring right at you.

"Heyyyy…" you say awkwardly.

They stare.

"Do you think I look more like mom or dad?" you ask, trying to make a joke.

But no one laughs.

Can endermen even laugh? You shiver a little at the thought.

When no one answers, you go to ask a question, "Why did you guys have my back like that?"

At the same time one of the endermen rasps at you, "*Who* are you?"

"You first," you say quickly.

One of the endermen blinks and then shrugs. "We like her, we didn't want you scaring her off by telling her that we were endermen. Villagers don't take kindly to that… freaks them out. Now… you."

"Um," you say. "I'm a zombie. Um, I made up that story about being your friends because I needed to find some endermen."

"You've found us…" the enderman said. "But why?"

Should you tell them the truth? Or is this your chance?

If you threaten to tell the old lady the truth if they don't give you their ender pearls, *turn to page 106*.

If you distract them by complimenting their appearances, *turn to page 104*.

You scan the horizon for the nearest trees. There aren't a lot in the area, not with the swamps and the lakes, but there are a couple a little ways off, and really... how many trees do you need to make a pickaxe.

You stumble off in the direction of the closest tree. When you get there, you wind up and take a swing at the trunk, just like you'd done countless times before.

Your fist hits the tree. *Blathwalap,* goes your fist. It is a strange wet sound. That seems a little *out of the ordinary.* But you ignore it and keep swinging.

Blathwalap, blathwalap, blathloop!

Nothing much seems to be happening.

You look at your fist. It's all beat out of shape.

What!

And that's when you remember! Zombies can't cut down trees! Zombie hands aren't good at doing much of anything. Even if you made a pickaxe, you wouldn't be able to hold it. And you definitely *can't* make a house.

"Dang," you say quietly.

Too afraid to return to the endermen empty-handed, you wander off into the rain. A little while later, a couple players building a tower spot you and snag you with a couple arrows before you can get away. Everything fades to black...

THE END

To go back a couple choices and try again, *turn to page 70.*

To go back to the moment you returned to the surface and choose a new direction, *turn to page 57.*

Or, flip to the beginning and choose a new story!

As you push cautiously through the door, you see something amazing. This room is totally covered in bright brilliant gold! The walls and ceiling and floor are all made from glorious gold blocks. You can feel the dollar signs flash in your eyes. This is a *jackpot!* Just think about all the awesome things that you could build out of this! *Think of all the powered rails you could build…*

You reach into your backpack for your pickaxe before realizing two very important things:

One, you don't have a pickaxe.

Two, you don't have a backpack.

Right.

Zombie.

You keep forgetting.

In the middle of the room, a large ornate altar (also made of gold, of course) stands proudly. There are a couple steps up and then at the top of the altar, a large chest sits. It seems somehow that this chest is caught in a beam of light that makes it stand out. Your eye keeps being drawn back to it. As you stare, you notice a tiny red spot above the lock of the chest. *What's that?*

You try to concentrate and look around the rest of the room. There's not a lot of other things here, except a fairly normal looking door at the other end of the room.

If you want to go through this door, *turn to page 61.*

If you want to open the chest, *turn to page 90.*

If you want to go back to the last room and take the right door, *turn to page 33.*

The thing is, you *can't pay*. If you were your own Minecraft character, of course you could pay. But when you woke up as a zombie, you had *nothing*. And you can't mine or anything. So, you still have exactly… nothing.

No, if you want those pearls, you're going to have to get them another way.

And you have an idea.

You twist your face into the best grimace you can manage, shake yourself from the old lady's grasp and run forward, yelling at the top of your lungs.

"Hippopotamus!" you yell, because you know it doesn't matter what you say.

The fear on Garbanzo's face is immediate. His face immediately goes white and he scrambles back, falling backwards off his chair and dropping the bag. Before it tumbles off the table, you wrap your green fingers around the bag.

Got it.

Garbanzo is screaming. He leaps up onto his bed and then without a pause he flies out the back door of the shack.

You turn quickly and head for the front door. You bust through it and head out into the night.

When you're almost out of the village, you hear a voice behind you, just audible through the pitter patter of the rain.

It's the old lady. She's standing at the door of the cottage.

"I was wrong, all zombies are the same," she says sadly. "Rotten flesh and rotten heart."

You stop. Your heart, rotten or not, sinks in your chest. You stare at the bag in your hand and then up at her.

"It's not like that—" you protest.

But she's not listening. "I made a mistake trusting you," she says. "I'm not going to let that happen again." And she turns and goes back in the cottage.

"I had to—" you say, but she's gone.

You wander through the night and find a little cave to hide in as the sun rises in the sky. You don't get a wink of sleep all day. You just can't stop thinking about the look on her face. It is seared in your mind. She was so disappointed, so hurt.

You try to tell yourself that she's just a character in the game. That she's not real. But aren't you just a character in this game now? Are you real?

You have no choice. When the sun sets, you head back in the direction that you came. You find the village and then the house on the outskirts of town. The lights are on and there are two voices speaking inside. *She's still here!*

And then you wait. You don't really have a plan, you just hope she comes out.

It's a little while later when the door swings open. You hear Garbanzo's voice. "I don't want to go out there, it's too dark. I'll get lost on the way to the well!"

You can hear the old lady click her tongue disapprovingly. "Give me the bucket," she says. "The night doesn't bother me. I can never see where I'm going anyways."

A second later, the old lady exits the door and feels her way to the end of the garden before turning right onto the road and towards the well.

You leave your hiding place and follow her down to the well. When she sinks her bucket into the well, you clear your throat behind her. "Hi," you say, "it's me."

The old lady drops the bucket and it rattles loudly inside the well. She turns quick. "Get away from me," she whispers sharply. "I'll scream!"

"No, I need you to listen to me for a second. I need to explain something," you plead.

She doesn't say anything but she also doesn't scream, so you take that as a good sign. "I'm sorry for lying to you, and I'm sorry for stealing from your friend. I know it was wrong, but, you see, I didn't have any other choice. I really needed these pearls. *Really.*"

"It was wrong," she says.

"I know, it was wrong. It was still wrong. But, here, this is what I wanted to tell you. This is going to be crazy, and you don't have to believe you, I just want you to hear it," you swallow hard. "Like I said, I need the pearls to get home, because I'm not from here. I'm not even really a zombie."

She doesn't seem too confused yet.

"I'm a kid, you see." You are talking softly and she leans forward to hear better. "I'm a kid from a different place. Like a different world. Where I'm from there are no zombies or skeletons or endermen. Things aren't made of blocks there. And there I play a game, it's called Minecraft, and that game takes place in this world. I fell asleep playing that game one night and when I woke, I was… this, a zombie, in this world!"

She doesn't say anything. She probably has no idea what you're talking about. You decide to finish the explanation anyways, it will make you feel better.

"An elder golem told me that there's been someone like this before and that to get back home they had to go to The End. I'm going there, but I need these pearls, and twelve blaze rods to get there. That's why I took them. And I'm sorry. But I'm scared, I don't belong here, and I don't know how else to get back."

You sigh deeply. "That probably sounds pretty crazy, huh?" you say with a little smile.

The woman looks at you with her unseeing eyes. "It doesn't sound that crazy," she says.

You're surprised, you take a step back. "I think that means that *you're* crazy," you joke.

She smiles. "No it doesn't sound that crazy, because I've heard it before, I think. Something just like it."

"What?" you ask bluntly.

"A long time ago," she says thoughtfully. "You know, I'm very old. *Very* old."

"How old?" you ask.

"No one really knows. I can't remember! Funnily enough, I'm too old to remember. But what I do remember is a young man just like you. He had a story just like yours that he told me one day…"

"The Elder Golem did say that there was one other. You met him?!" You grab her shoulder. "What happened to him?"

"I met him," she says. "He was quite nice. He had a funny name… I can't remember. Oh, yes, Notch, or something like that. Anyways, I'm not sure what happened to him. I think he got home. He had many people helping him. He helped everyone and so we all helped him get home."

"Notch?" you repeat, dumbfounded.

"Yeah," she smiles. "A funny name, isn't it?"

Notch, you think, *the creator of Minecraft…* You get lost in the wonderings. *Why was he here? Better question: why am I here? What do I have in common with Notch?*

"Come on," says the old woman, "let's go."

You shake your head to clear your mind. "Where?" you ask dumbly.

"Home," she says with a smile. "You have to get home. And to get there, you need to visit the Nether. And I think I know something that might help."

"Come on," she says again, walking away into the night.

You stumble after her, towards home, towards the Nether, and towards your next adventure.

THE END

Congratulations, you've reached one of the three happiest endings of this story. The story continues in The Zombie Adventure 3: Plunge into the Nether, available now! There are two other endings in this book that lead to the next book in the series. Can you find them? To go back to the last choice and try again, turn to page 34, or turn to page 57 to go to the moment you returned to the surface and head off in a different direction, or flip to the beginning and choose a new story!

Hi Reader,

Thanks so much for reading! I hope you really enjoyed this book!

Would you do me a favour? It's tough getting started as a new author. Even if your book is really good, there are hundreds of books online and people might not be able to find yours. But you can help me with this. **If you leave a review on my book, it will help other people find it, and will let me know that you want me to write more!**

It doesn't have to be a long review or well-written. Just search for *Zombie Adventure 2* on Amazon and click on this book. Scroll down and click on 'Write a Customer Review', click on the stars and write a couple words about what you thought of the book. It would mean so much to me! Thank you!

If you want to find out more about me and my books you can go to **johndiary.com**.

If you want to read more Choose Your Own Stories, you can get a free Choose Your Own Story book when you join my fan club at johndiary.com/signup. Just put in your e-mail address and I'll send you a book for free. Also I'll send you free previews of my books when they come out! And get the chance to win future books!

Flip to the back of the book to see sneak peeks of my other books!

You can also keep up with me online:

Facebook: John Diary at facebook.com/johndiarybooks

Twitter: @johndiarybooks

Instagram: johndiarybooks

Keep reading! Keep choosing!

You're the best,

John Diary

"Hey, guys, you really do look great," you say. "And anyways, it doesn't really matter what you look like. Being wonderful on the inside is going to make you and the people around you a *lot* happier."

"But look at my nose!" one of them says. "It's ugly!" This enderman is staring deep into the orb so that it's almost touching their face.

You don't even have *a nose,* you think.

"You know, all this staring in the mirror really isn't any good for you," you say. "It just makes you obsessed with the way you look. It makes you see every little flaw and criticize it. When you look at yourself that close, all you can see are the bad details and not the amazing whole."

A couple of the endermen lower their pearls and look at you. They don't seem convinced.

You point to one of them. "How do you feel when you're looking in the orb?"

The enderman stares at their feet.

"Do you feel *good?*" you ask.

"No," the enderman says quietly.

"Do you feel bad?"

"Yeah."

Now they're all staring at you.

"But I just can't help it!" the enderman says. "I have to look at myself!"

You shake your head. "Well, I mean," you say, sounding hesitant. "I guess I could help you…"

"Yeah?" the enderman asks hopefully.

"I could take the orb off your hands. I'll take them so that you can't look at yourself. It'll make you happier," you sigh, as if this were really hard.

"Really?" the enderman says. "You'd do that?"

"Yeah, of course! For you… anything," you say with a quiet smile.

Hesitantly the enderman hands over their pearl. You try to take it from them, but for a second they cling to it and then let go.

"Well done," you say.

"I already feel lighter!" the enderman said helpfully.

"Will you help me?" another enderman asks.

"Of course," you say, trying to suppress your giant smile.

"Me too!" another one chimes in.

"Help me!" says another raspy voice.

A couple minutes later you are cradling thirteen pearls in your arms.

"Thanks guys," you say.

"Thank you!" they say.

"I suppose I should take her back to her village now," you say nodding at the old lady.

"Hey, Rotney," one of them says as you turn to leave. "Now you really *are* family. Come back whenever."

You smile. "Thanks guys."

You walk over to the edge of the roof where the old lady's standing. "Hey, let me take you back," you say.

"Thanks," she says, but there's something funny about her face.

"No worries," you say distractedly.

She grabs your arm and the two of you head back down and towards the far away village.

She doesn't talk at all through the long walk.

Halfway through, you can't take it anymore. "What's going on?" you ask.

She stops walking. "Why'd you lie to me?"

"What?" you say, your heart dropping in your chest. You were in such a good mood. You got the pearls. Did you even really lie?!

The woman turns to you, pain creases her face. "You lied. You said they were your friends. But then you said they were your family. Why weren't you honest with me?"

"I, uh— I…" You don't know what to say. She doesn't even know *half* the lies you told. There's something about the way that she's looking at you that completely breaks your heart. You realize that you only have these pearls because she helped you. You owe her everything. The least you can give her is the truth.

"I'm sorry," you say. "I did lie. I actually lied more than you know."

She purses her lips, disappointed.

"They're not my friends—"

"I know," she spits.

You nod, feeling terrible. "But they're also not my family."

Her eyebrows form an angry 'v'.

"There's a lot to explain, butI couldn't tell you the truth, because I thought you'd be scared: I'm not a villager, I'm not like you. I'm a… zombie."

She took a couple steps back, fear dashing across her face.

"That's why my voice is so weird," you say. "It's cause I'm talking zombie. Just like the people you met before. They were zombies too! But you understand us, because unlike other villagers you don't run the minute you meet us!"

She nods, thinking about it. "That's why everyone else ran…" she says. "I understand. But what I don't understand is why you had to lie about them, why were you looking for them anyways?"

"Because they're not villagers either. They're endermen. They didn't want you to know because they thought you'd be scared and wouldn't visit them anymore."

She raises her eyebrows. "You're really blowing my mind today."

You smile. "Yeah," you say. "I thought you might know some endermen who you didn't know were endermen and I needed to find them for the pearls."

She nods. "I see, so you lied."

You stare at the ground, not sure what to say.

She grabs your arm. "Let's go."

You take a couple steps forward. "You forgive me?"

"Hmmm," she says. "Maybe. You're not lying anymore?" She looks at you.

You swallow. "I'm, uh, I'm not telling you the whole truth." You can't help yourself. You can't hurt this old lady anymore.

She raises her eyebrows again. "What else is there?"

"This is going to be crazy, and you don't have to believe you, I just want you to hear it, I want to be honest with you." You swallow hard. "Like I said, I need the pearls to get home, because I'm not from here. I'm not even actually a zombie."

"Are you a zombie or not a zombie? I can't keep up!" she exclaims.

"I'm a…. kid, you see." You are talking softly and she leans forward to hear better. "I'm a kid from a different place. Like a different world. Where I'm from there are no zombies or skeletons or endermen. Things aren't made of blocks there. And there I play a game, it's called Minecraft, and that game takes place in this world. I fell asleep playing that game one night and when I woke, I was… this! A zombie! In this world!"

She doesn't say anything. She probably has no idea what you're talking about. You decide to finish the explanation anyways, it will make you feel better.

"An elder golem told me that there's been someone like this before and that to get back home they had to go to The End. I'm going there, but I need these pearls, and twelve blaze rods to get there. That's why I lied to you. And I'm sorry. But I'm scared, I don't belong here, and I don't know how else to get back."

You sigh deeply. "That probably sounds pretty crazy, huh?" you say with a little smile.

The woman looks at you with her unseeing eyes. "It doesn't sound that crazy," she says.

You're surprised, you take a step back. "I think that means that *you're* crazy," you joke.

She smiles. "No it doesn't sound that crazy, because I've heard it before, I think. Something just like it."

"What?" you ask bluntly.

"A long time ago," she says thoughtfully. "You know, I'm very old. *Very* old."

"How old?" you ask.

"No one really knows. I can't remember! Funnily enough, I'm so old, that I've forgotten. But what I do remember is a young man just like you. He had a story just like yours that he told me one day…"

"The Elder Golem did say that there was one other. You met him?!" You grab her shoulder. "What happened to him?"

"I met him," she says. "He was quite nice. He had a funny name... I can't remember. Oh, yes, Notch, or something like that. Anyways, I'm not sure what happened to him. I think he got home. He had many people helping him. He helped everyone and so we all helped him get home."

"Notch?" you repeat, dumbfounded.

"Yeah," she smiles. "A funny name, isn't it?"

Notch, you think, *the creator of Minecraft...* You get lost in the wonderings. *Why was he here? Better question: why am I here? What do I have to do with Notch?*

"Come on," says the old woman, "let's go."

You shake your head to clear your mind. "Where?" you ask dumbly.

"Home," she says with a smile. "You have to get home. And to get there, you need to visit the Nether. And I think I know something that might help."

"Come on," she says again, walking away into the wild.

You stumble after her, towards home, towards the Nether, and towards your next adventure.

THE END

Congratulations, you've reached one of the three happiest endings of this story. The story continues in The Zombie Adventure 3: Plunge into the Nether, available now! There are two other endings in this book that lead to the next book in the series. Can you find them? To go back to the last choice and try again, turn to page 104, or turn to page 57 to go to the moment you returned to the surface and head off in a different direction, or flip to the beginning and choose a new story!

Hi Reader,

Thanks so much for reading! I hope you really enjoyed this book!

Would you do me a favour? It's tough getting started as a new author. Even if your book is really good, there are hundreds of books online and people might not be able to find yours. But you can help me with this. **If you leave a review on my book, it will help other people find it, and will let me know that you want me to write more!**

It doesn't have to be a long review or well-written. Just search for *Zombie Adventure 2* on Amazon and click on this book. Scroll down and click on 'Write a Customer

Review', click on the stars and write a couple words about what you thought of the book. It would mean so much to me! Thank you!

If you want to find out more about me and my books you can go to **johndiary.com.**

If you want to read more Choose Your Own Stories, you can get a free Choose Your Own Story book when you join my fan club at johndiary.com/signup. Just put in your e-mail address and I'll send you a book for free. Also I'll send you free previews of my books when they come out! And get the chance to win future books!

Flip to the back of the book to see sneak peeks of my other books!

You can also keep up with me online:

Facebook: John Diary at facebook.com/johndiarybooks

Twitter: @johndiarybooks

Instagram: johndiarybooks

Keep reading! Keep choosing!

You're the best,

John Diary

"They'll pay rent!" you blurt out. It's the first thing you could think of.

She almost laughs. "The endermen will pay rent?"

"Yes, I promise!" you beg.

"I don't know… it would have to be pretty good to convince the town to let some freaky endermen in…"

"Oh, they'd pay very well!" you say, thinking fast. "Very well."

The old lady raises her eyebrows as if to say, *'How much?'*

"They'll pay…" and that's when it hits you. "They'll pay in emeralds. How does twenty three blocks of emerald ore, dropped in the town square, every storm, sound?"

She is speechless. When she finally opens her mouth to speak she is interrupted by a roar from behind you. It's a hoard of angry villagers.

"GET AWAY FROM GRANDMA MOLE," the leader of the hoard yells, "YOU MONSTER!"

The villagers are waving weapons and tools viciously.

"No, no, I'm not attacking her," you say in a panic. You turn to the old lady. "Tell them that I'm not hurting you! Tell them what I said!"

She bites her lip and then turns to the fast-approaching crowd. She raises her hands. "Stop! He's not a monster! He's got a deal for us!"

The villagers stop suddenly.

"A deal?" the leader asks, his hoe still waving in the air.

"A very good deal," the woman says.

The villagers lower their weapons slowly. The woman tells them what you've just said. They grumble and shriek when she mentions the endermen but when she mentions the twenty-three emerald ore, they all fall silent.

"So?" she says. "What do you think?"

"So?" you ask.

The leader turns to the rest of the village. They're waiting for him to speak.

The leader furrows his brow, itches his long nose and then smiles. "I think we're RICH!"

The villagers all throw their weapons in the air in celebration. The weapons come raining back down to a chorus of *ows*.

"Go tell them," the old woman says.

And with a smile on your face, you turn and march off into the wilderness.

You hurry to the arch, and then to the hill underneath it.

One of the endermen spots you and calls out to his brothers and sisters. They look a little surprised.

"We didn't think we'd ever see you again. We thought you'd be a zombie-kebab by now!" the enderman says as you approach.

You smile. "Nope, I'm back, and I have good news."

You tell them that it's all worked out, you can use the house at the outskirts when it's raining. They'll have to cram in, but they'll be dry.

"Amazing!" the enderman says. "We'll teleport over there now!"

"Great," you say. "And one more thing, when you do go over, the villagers would like you to bring one of those shiny green rocks with you. They want to decorate their village with it."

"One of these?" an enderman says, holding out emerald ore as if it was just a little disgusting. "Villagers are weird."

Each enderman grabs a piece of emerald ore. "We're ready to go," says one of the endermen. "Oh but before we go, here's these."

Twelve endermen stride forward and shake until a little pearl falls on the ground. "Thanks strange zombie, we'll think of you each time it rains!" And with that, the endermen snap out of existence.

You gather up the pearls, and with a smile on your face and no idea of where to go next, you start walking towards the town. Maybe you'll just check to make sure everything worked out okay.

As you reach the outskirts of town, you spot one house that is further away than the others. You peer in the window and see twenty-three endermen packed in there like sardines. You laugh a little and keep walking. Most of the villagers are freaking out over a stack of emerald ore in the middle of town.

Your job here is done. You choose a direction and start walking.

But out of the corner of your eye, you see some movement. At the edge of the village, the old woman is standing with a younger villager who is pointing at you excitedly.

What now? Are they going to attack you again? You start walking quicker but a second later you hear a voice yell out at you. "Stop, Mr. Zombie sir! Grandma Mole wants to talk to you!"

You stop. "What?"

The younger villager stops, panting. "Grandma Mole, she wants to speak to you."

Why? You're intrigued, so you let the villager show you back to the village where the old lady is waiting for you.

"Hello," she says.

"Hi?" you say. "What did you want?"

"That's not a very polite thing to say," Grandma Mole scolds.

It feels like your grandma getting mad at you, you hang your head in shame. "Sorry," you say.

"I wanted to ask you something." She dismisses the other villager. "They tell me that you're a… zombie? No one else can understand you? But I… can. There's something special about you. Who are you?"

You feel sweat pooling under your shirt. She's onto you.

"I'm just a zombie," you say.

"You're lying," she says. "I'm blind, but I wasn't born yesterday. I know when people are lying to me."

You feel bad. She saved your life, and helped you get these pearls. You do owe her something.

"Tell me who you are…" she says. "I have to know, I—" There's something that she's not saying.

"Okay, I will, you say, but you're not going to believe me," you swallow hard. "You see, I'm not even really a zombie."

She squints at you. It feels good to tell someone the truth.

"I'm a kid, you see." You are talking softly and she leans forward to hear better. "I'm a kid from a different place. Like a different world. Where I'm from there are no zombies or skeletons or endermen. Things aren't made of blocks there. And there I play a game, it's called Minecraft, and that game takes place in *this* world. I fell asleep playing that game one night and when I woke, I was… this, a zombie, in this world!" She doesn't say anything. She probably has no idea what you're talking about. You decide to finish the explanation anyways, it will make you feel better.

"An elder golem told me that there's been someone like this before and that to get back home they had to go to The End. I'm going there, but I needed twelve ender pearls, and twelve blaze rods to get there. That's why I made this deal with you, so that the endermen would pay me in ender pearls."

You sigh deeply. "That probably sounds pretty crazy, huh?" you say with a little smile.

The woman looks at you with her unseeing eyes. "It doesn't sound that crazy," she says.

You're surprised, you take a step back. "I think that means that *you're* crazy," you joke.

She smiles. "No it doesn't sound that crazy, because I've heard it before, I think. Something just like it."

"What?" you ask bluntly.

"A long time ago," she says thoughtfully. "You know, I'm very old. *Very* old."

"How old?" you ask.

"No one really knows. I can't remember! Funnily enough, I'm too old to remember. But what I do remember is a young man just like you. He had a story just like yours that he told me one day…"

"The Elder Golem did say that there was one other. You met him?!" You grab her shoulder. "What happened to him?"

"I met him," she says. "He was quite nice. He had a funny name… I can't remember. Oh, yes, Notch, or something like that. Anyways, I'm not sure what happened to him. I think he got home. He had many people helping him. He helped everyone and so we all helped him get home."

"Notch?" you repeat, dumbfounded.

"Yeah," she smiles. "A funny name, isn't it?"

Notch, you think, *the creator of Minecraft…* You get lost in the wonderings. *Why was he here? Better question: why am I here? What do I have to do with Notch?*

"Come on," says the old woman, "let's go."

You shake your head to clear your mind. "Where?" you ask dumbly.

"Home," she says with a smile. "You have to get home. And to get there, you need to visit the Nether. And I think I know something that might help."

"Come on," she says again, walking away into the village.

You stumble after her, towards home, towards the Nether, and towards your next adventure.

THE END

Congratulations, you've reached one of the three happiest endings of this story. This story continues in The Zombie Adventure 3: Plunge into the Nether, available now! There are two other endings in this book that lead to the next book in the series. Can you find them? To go back to the last choice and try again, turn to page 77, or turn to page 57 to go to the moment you returned to the surface and head off in a different direction, or flip to the beginning and choose a new story!

Hi Reader,

Thanks so much for reading! I hope you really enjoyed this book!

Would you do me a favour? It's tough getting started as a new author. Even if your book is really good, there are hundreds of books online and people might not be able to find yours. But you can help me with this. **If you leave a review on my book, it will help other people find it, and will let me know that you want me to write more!**

It doesn't have to be a long review or well-written. Just search for *Zombie Adventure 2* on Amazon and click on this book. Scroll down and click on 'Write a Customer Review', click on the stars and write a couple words about what you thought of the book. It would mean so much to me! Thank you!

If you want to find out more about me and my books you can go to

johndiary.com.

If you want to read more Choose Your Own Stories, you can get a free Choose Your Own Story book when you join my fan club at johndiary.com/signup. Just put in your e-mail address and I'll send you a book for free. Also I'll send you free previews of my books when they come out! And get the chance to win future books!

Flip to the back of the book to see sneak peeks of my other books!

You can also keep up with me online:

Facebook: John Diary at facebook.com/johndiarybooks

Twitter: @johndiarybooks

Instagram: johndiarybooks

Keep reading! Keep choosing!

You're the best,

John Diary

If you liked this book, you'll love the heart-warming and gut-busting tale of Sneezy Steve. He has just spawned in the world of Minecraft with nothing: no memories, no items and no clue what to do next. The only thing he does have is a mysterious photograph of a girl with orange hair in the bottom of his backpack.

What happens next? I can't even say, because it's all up to you. Will Steve ask a sheep for directions? Will he become best friends with an old block of dirt? Maybe you'll help him look for the girl in the photograph. Or maybe you'll not be so helpful and turn him into a zombie, or make him pretend to be a wolf. The choice is yours in my brand new series!

Dan is playing Minecraft with his friends, like he always does, when a strange figure, white from head-to-toe, approaches him in the game and drops a book at his feet. Cautiously, Dan reads the book: it's an invitation, to a school. A school for only the very best Minecraft players in the country.

It all seems to good to be true.

And maybe it is…

CHOOSE YOUR OWN MINECRAFT STORY

THE ZOMBIE ADVENTURE 3

PLUNGE INTO THE NETHER

JOHN DIARY

Your story continues in the land of stone and flame that they call the Nether! As you search for the blaze rods you need to finish the End portal, your path might cross a bunch of very bored blazes with some anger management problems, or make you chief of a kingdom of zombie pigmen! Maybe you'll go to war, or just get them to build a big pyramid for you to hang out on. But the most dangerous person you'll meet of all of them is a not-so-smart villager, who just can't seem to leave you alone!

Made in the USA
Coppell, TX
08 December 2021

67646916R00081